CW01374064

HONEY TRAP MARKETING

The 5-Step Formula
to Magnetizing Your Ideal Buyers
in Less than 2 Hours Per Week

DEIRDRE TSHIEN

COPYRIGHT 2022 BY DEIRDRE TSHIEN
ALL RIGHTS RESERVED
NO PART OF THIS PUBLICATION MAY BE REPLICATED,
DUPLICATED OR REPUBLISHED WITHOUT THE
WRITTEN PERMISSION OF DEIRDRE TSHIEN
ISBN: 9798831603705
Imprint: Independently published

DEDICATION

To my husband & best friend, Ash,
my co-founder & partner-in-crime, Bona,
the only ones crazy enough to follow me
to NYC based only on our dreams.

TABLE OF CONTENTS

FOREWORD I

1. HONEY TRAP MARKETING 1

An Experimental… 8
Heart-Centered Approach… 12
… To Rapidly Converting Followers into Buyers… 15

2. THE HONEY TRAP FORMULA 19

3. CUTTING-THROUGH WITH YOUR MESSAGING 22

What's Their Before and After? 25
How Can You Use Data to Determine Your Winning Messages? ... 35

4. CREATING YOUR CONTENT HONEY TRAPS 42

How Do We Tap into Our Audience's Emotions? 47
How Do We Master the Art of Storytelling? 49
How Do We Provide Practical Value? 64
Creating Your Content Honey Traps 65
Accelerating Your Content Honey Traps (In Less Than 5 Mins a Week) 69
How to Create Posts That Will Stop the Scroll 70

5. BUILDING YOUR TRIBE WITH THE TRAFFIC PYRAMID 74

But first... Where Do I Build My Tribe? 79
Tier 2: Active Organic Marketing 81
Tier 3: Leveraging Other People's Audiences 102
Tier 4: Scaling with Paid Ads 119

6. LEADING YOUR TRIBE INTO THE SALE 124

What are Lead Attracting Conversion Events? 125
Which Strategy is Right for You? 164

7. DOING IT ALL WHILE SPENDING ONLY 2 HOURS PER WEEK ON SOCIAL MEDIA! 171

The Delegation Mindset 172
Building Your Habits 183

SUMMARY 187

ABOUT THE AUTHOR 189

FOREWORD

As a serial entrepreneur, who started at the age of seven selling my buddy's drawings on the school playground and turned my little business that I ran out of my apartment into a multi-million-dollar consulting, coaching and software empire, I've seen *everything* there is to see when it comes to marketing.

As a goat farmer from Wisconsin who was featured in Forbes for being able to charge up to $2,500 per book, I've figured out what it takes to be real and build an authentic brand.

And as someone who hates theory-spewers (you know those people who publish crap that sounds great but they don't even know if it works!) I've BS-checked every sales and marketing strategy and tactic out there.

So, when I met Deirdre and learned about her Honey Trap Marketing strategy, I realized Deirdre had somehow managed to distill and join the dots on all the necessary (and often overlooked!) parts of digital marketing into one neat framework.

It is one of those rare strategies that *actually works* for *any* industry. For action takers that is!

There is so much more to marketing than people realize but most people also overcomplicate it at the same time.

A lot of entrepreneurs overvalue the desire to get known, and waste lots of time and money on "brand awareness" with no idea how to turn these eyeballs into customers!

Other entrepreneurs try to get clever with different ways of getting visibility on all the social media platforms and ironically end up going down all these random rabbit holes instead of showing up for their audience.

And then we have the entrepreneurs who are so hyper-focused on sales that they skip the whole marketing and lead generation part and wonder why the heck they aren't getting the conversions they want!

The thing is, each of these things is important.

Getting known. Getting seen. Getting leads (and sales!)

But you can't have one without the others.

And there is a smart *strategic* way to get it all for your business.

That way is Honey Trap Marketing. And this book is your playbook to mastering it.

Dana Derricks

1.
HONEY TRAP MARKETING

"THE TRAIN IS TERMINATING AT THIS STATION."

"THE TRAIN IS TERMINATING AT THIS STATION."

The loudspeaker jolted me awake and I sat up trying to get my bearings together. I had a sinking feeling in the pit of my stomach it had finally happened. I had taken it too far and had ended up at the end of the line. Literally and figuratively.

It was at this point that I knew things had to change. I had been going for too long feeling this sheer exhaustion.

While it was easy for me to palm it off as the mental and physical exhaustion that comes with having a corporate 9-5 job and a pretty physical new business in hospitality where the struggle to be Chief Everything Officer was real… I knew this wasn't the *true* source of my exhaustion.

The true source of my exhaustion was stemming from the seemingly never-ending internal conflicts that were going on in my mind. The constant second-guessing. The endless excuses I was making. And the drain that *all* of that was having on my energy and my emotional state.

It was at this point - when I found myself at the end of the train line - that I knew I had to stop giving into my own BS.

My own BS that I already knew everything, so why listen to others who have been there and done that?

My own BS that I could do everything, so why try to create focus?

My own BS about truly connecting with our audience… Why bother wasting their time about who we are when they just need to know about what we're selling?

My own BS that our people - our true buyers - will come and seek us out, so why bother wasting time trying to find *them*?

My own BS that no one can do the job as well as I can, so why bother even trying to systemize and delegate? In fact, that would actually mean *more* of my time and energy to create those systems and find someone to delegate to in the first place!

Phew! Are you just as exhausted reading about my BS as I am writing about them?

And do you know why? Because I bet that at some point, one or more of these excuses have come up for you as well.

I know this because if you're reading this book, then you're most likely like me - smart, intelligent, capable, driven, ambitious, filled with unfulfilled potential.

And if you *are* anything like me, then you're probably also filled with a fire and a need to prove yourself.

The good news is that I am going to be laying it all out for you inside this book. All of my struggles, my wins, my tactics, my mindset, my self-talk and all the things my team and I do day in, day out NOW to win and keep winning…

It all comes down to ONE strategy.

The one strategy that I have seen emerge over and over across all of my different businesses, that I have built into multiple 6 and 7-figures.

The one strategy that I will completely lay out for you in this book.

The one strategy that if you can understand and fully implement (just do what I tell you on these subsequent pages!) - you will be able to level up and reach those sales goals for your business.

The one strategy that will help you finally fulfil your potential and be the person you knew you were put on this earth to be.

That strategy?

Honey Trap Marketing.

Let me rewind a little and explain how this all came about.

I still remember the moment my husband and I made the decision to go "all-in."

I was sitting on the couch watching TV and could hear Ash in the kitchen singing off-beat as he checked on his latest dessert creation.

The sweet aroma of baked chocolate from the open oven drifted into the living room. It made my shoulders relax and my mouth salivate, even though we had just finished eating dinner.

Ash had discovered a love of baking and was using it as a way to escape from his unhappiness at school. He was studying medicine and the workload was all-consuming, the content dry and the hospitals sterile.

Dessert brought me the kind of joy that allowed me to temporarily forget about my disillusioned dreams of climbing the corporate ladder. Coming from an Asian family with strict expectations, I was following the "go to school, get spotless grades, get a good job" model, and it was draining my soul.

Those moments felt especially precious to both Ash and I because they were like a "time-out" from the hamster wheel - the perpetual cycle of work that seemed to be void of meaning and purpose.

Have you ever felt like that?

We were both unhappy in what we were doing, and had been talking on and off about potentially starting a business. But what could we do? How would we get started? When?

We had very little money, no ideas, no connections or business skills, and other than our desire to escape our current situation: we had no clue what to do.

Ash brought his new dessert creation into the living room. He had been working like a mad scientist, perfecting my all-time favorite dessert - a dessert we used to travel half an hour to eat in a small, rustic Italian restaurant in Sydney. My jaw dropped as he entered the room and finally presented it.

It was a chocolate molten lava cake; a divine expression of otherworldly deliciousness that, when eaten, could ascend you to a higher plane of enlightenment. And it did!

It was over that particular dessert - which we ultimately named The Choc Pot - when we made the decision to embark on our entrepreneurial journey. In that delicious moment of chocolatey heaven, we committed to opening our own dessert bar, taking Sydney by storm!

Now… did it quite pan out that way?

In some ways, yes. In a lot of ways, no.

Let me fast forward a couple of years into having launched The Choc Pot and unfortunately, I was still working in my corporate job. Given the debt we were already in with our initial store, and the plans we had that year of opening another 2-3 stores, we couldn't afford for me to quit yet.

So, I was still working in an investment bank in Sydney and it was around this time that I had joined a new team. A team where I only knew one other person. To bring us all together, our manager arranged a meet-and-greet event, so we could get to know each other.

It was a sunny, warm day in Sydney and I was standing on the balcony with two other members of my new team. James was the one person I already knew because we were acquaintances who had hung out in similar circles during University. Nic, I didn't know at all, but I remember how animated he was. He had us in tears, laughing.

As we were chatting, Nic suddenly turned to us and said, "Oh, I went to this amazing place last night with some friends. It was started by this couple. The guy was studying medicine and wasn't enjoying it, but he loved baking and was perfecting this dessert, called a choc pot, for his girlfriend. And from that they started this business. Isn't that so cool?!"

I was incredibly embarrassed because as the type of introvert who finds any excuse to blend into the background, I hated that type of attention (even though at the time he didn't know I was the girlfriend in the story)!

Of course, James wasn't going to let it go. He knew me, our story, and turned to Nic saying, "Yeah Nic, don't you know it's her?" He was pointing at me! I'm pretty sure I was smiling awkwardly, shifting from foot to foot, avoiding eye contact, and I don't blame Nic for being totally confused.

Then, Nic tried being helpful by clarifying: "I'm talking about this couple. He was studying medicine and gave it up so that they could start a dessert bar. It's called The Choc Pot. You guys have to go try it!" James pointed at me again, and emphasized, "Yeah dude! It's her!"

When Nic finally realized what James was saying, he was gaping at me in wonder. "I know all about your story! It's so inspiring what you've done and we love The Choc Pot!"

Even though I genuinely appreciated and was flattered by what Nic was saying, I simultaneously wanted the ground to open and swallow me up so I could get away from the attention (see what I mean about the sheer exhaustion?).

Looking back, what I particularly love about this story with Nic is that, without even realizing it at the time, we had *become known* and had someone literally standing in front of me raving about us, selling us to other people!

It was the in-person version of the constant notifications that had been coming through on my phone and email, saying so and so has mentioned The Choc Pot on Instagram, on Facebook, in reviews, in blog posts - again and again. Because…

We were now KNOWN!

Everyone wanted a piece of it! We had people coming in ordering off *just* our social media or email. They wouldn't even look at the menu! We had people coming in saying they were trying us out because their friends told them to. We had more and more people coming in and bringing more and more of their friends and families.

And we still kept getting notifications on social media of people sharing our stuff, posting more stuff, tagging us. It was insane!

I knew then that we were definitely on to something.

So, I re-looked at everything we had been doing and all the things I had been learning from other businesses at the time - and I saw a pattern.

Time and again, we kept coming back to 3 fundamental principles.

Every time I was stuck, I came back to these principles.

Every time I didn't know what to do next, I came back to these principles.

Every time I needed to make a step-change; I came back to these principles.

Which is why these principles are the cornerstones of Honey Trap Marketing **- an experimental, heart-centered approach to rapidly converting followers into buyers**.

Honey Trap Marketing is how you are going to ethically "trap" your buyer with something so sweet and sticky and pleasurable that they *willingly* become raving fans.

Let me tell you, in coming up with this definition, I *agonized* over the particular words to use. Because it is SO much harder to try to be succinct and come up with a one-liner than it is to write two full pages explaining Honey Trap Marketing. So, the words chosen were very deliberate.

For example, notice that we start with **experimental** and **heart-centered**. Two very different and almost contradictory words that are speaking to both the scientific and artistic approach we must have to marketing.

I cannot stress enough how important it is for you - as an entrepreneur - to be able to know, do and implement *both*. Doing one may provide the traps, but not the honey. Or it may provide the honey and not the traps. When you can do both? Then you've got Honey Traps!

In many larger businesses with dedicated marketing teams, you might notice that there are specialist roles in Performance Marketing (people who can read the data and make recommendations on changes to be made) and Creative, Design and Copy (people who create the creatives and write the copy for content, ads, etc.) - because ordinarily, it is difficult for any one person to be able to master both.

However, as entrepreneurs, we are not ordinary. In fact, by having made the crazy decision to take this big risk and try to build something of our own (with extremely limited resources), we are incredibly *extraordinary*. Which is why mastering BOTH the art and the science that comes with the territory of entrepreneurship.

And that is why Honey Trap Marketing must encompass both. It is the only way you can get results as quickly as possible! And that is what I am here to help you with - to get results as quickly as possible!

With that said, let's dive into each of the 3 fundamental principles of Honey Trap Marketing so you have the complete understanding of *what* it is before we get into the *how*.

An Experimental...

Did you ever sit in science class in high school and wonder why the heck we were learning this stuff? Who cares about what happens when you mix potassium with chlorine? Or how quickly dyed water moves up a celery stick? Or why it is it that only opposite poles have magnetic attraction?

Well, I'm not too proud to say that I now need to eat my words. Because in hindsight, what science was teaching us wasn't necessarily the ins and outs of the periodic table (although it sure felt like it!), but rather the *approach* we should be taking to everything we do in business - and especially in our marketing.

The only certainty we have in this world is uncertainty. The only constant in our lives is change. And the only way we can navigate all of this uncertainty and change to have our marketing work without losing our sanity is through *experimentation*.

Because one of the two ways we make sense of our lives is through a fundamental scientific principle: cause-and-effect (I'll be taking you through the second way in the next section!).

What we were really learning in those hard-to-sit-through 7th grade classes was cause and effect.

For example, whenever seeds are planted in soil, when they germinate, the roots grow downwards and stems grow upwards - the result of gravity (the cause) affecting the plant auxins (the effect).

Or that the way the earth, moon and sun are positioned (the cause) will actually impact how the moon looks at each of its phases (the effect).

Or that it actually matters the degrees to which you nail pieces of wood together for a trebuchet (the cause) for it to actually catapult (the effect).

And the only way we can track these effects in each experiment is through... **data**.

DATA

The data tells us where we need to focus for our "traps". Without focus, your ability to get things done - let alone the right things done for your marketing - greatly diminishes.

Is this something you're potentially struggling with right now?

Because trust me when I say I get it. When I started The Choc Pot, I was doing ALL of the things to the point I had absolutely no focus and all I really had to show for it was sheer exhaustion.

When I was working in banking, a lot of what I did was analysis work. Lots and lots of numbers and data. Before I had joined the new team I had previously mentioned, I was actually working on this particular project analyzing the revenue model for a product the bank owned.

All I knew was the outcome the CEO wanted - 10x more revenue from that product. This was the effect we were all looking for. We just needed to find the right cause(s).

We started building the model around the particular levers we knew we could pull to create this outcome. We focused on the number of new customers, number of retained customers, and price. Those were the drivers of revenue for that product, which meant that we had focus.

We knew what we needed to actually focus on because the data would tell us. The number of new customers were still increasing, our retained customers were holding if not increasing slightly, but our pricing had been the same for years. I started to model the pricing and the impact on revenue that *if nothing else changed*, what an increase in pricing would have on revenue. And it was a lot.

We made the change in pricing, and revenue from that product immediately 10x'd overnight.

The only way you can create focus is by using the data to find the causes for the effect. And experiment until you create changes in the data you are looking for.

However, please keep in mind that this is just one side of the coin - the science. Because again, if you're anything like me, then you've probably been told before how important the data is. You've probably tried looking at it, and your eyes and mind went blurry, hazy, perhaps just left your body because you had no idea what you were even looking at!

And that's where the art comes in. In order for you to be able to succeed in your marketing with the data, you need the stories. Remember when I told you that Cause and Effect was one of the two ways we make sense of our lives? The other way we make sense of our lives is through Stories.

Stories *behind* the data AND stories *in front of* the data.

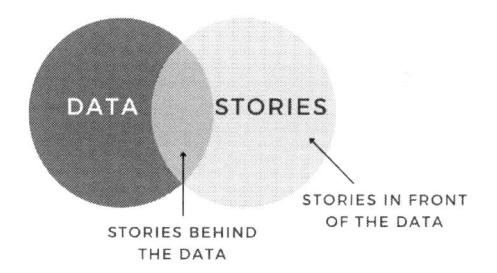

So, what the heck do I mean by these?

Stories fundamentally create *connection*.

Stories BEHIND the data create connections between the data and *the action you need to take.*

Stories IN FRONT OF the data create connections between these actions and your audience.

DATA → ACTION → AUDIENCE

STORIES BEHIND THE DATA (between DATA and ACTION)

STORIES IN FRONT OF THE DATA (between ACTION and AUDIENCE)

Let me explain what I mean.

Who here can look at a dump of data from say your Instagram account or from your Facebook ads account and *not know what the heck you're even looking at?*

You know why? Because the data first needs to be translated. We need to be able to read it in a way where we can find the causal linkages, where we can create a hypothesis about what the causes are and what we need to change in order to create the effect. These stories are required in all of our experiments, because THIS is how the data focuses our actions.

The stories behind the data will actually tell you where you need to focus your actions. So, the data tells you what you need to focus on, and the stories behind the data will tell you what actions you probably need to be taking.

And a lot of knowing those stories and those actions is going to come from common sense, from being told by people with experience, and from your own experimentation. Just starting with a hypothesis about something, trying it and seeing if the metrics moved how you expected it to.

This is what I mean by the stories BEHIND the data.

And then in taking that action, when it comes to your marketing, chances are it's going to come down to the stories in FRONT of the data. Because now you need to connect with your audience. You need to become *sticky*.

Enter, the…

Heart-Centered Approach…

The first time I ever heard this term, I actually didn't know what it actually meant. In practice. It seems a little embarrassing saying that now, but honestly, I think I knew intellectually what it meant, which is what I thought I was being…

Until I realized I wasn't. At least not completely.

It wasn't that I was lying, it's just that I didn't know how to *be*.

I call this period in my business my Business Mid-Life Crisis.

Let me tell you about it…

Since opening our first ever The Choc Pot store, we had built it into a multiple 7-figure business and had grown it to 5 locations. We had also started and built another 7-figure business - a burger restaurant called Stax On Burgers alongside it (of which we grew to 2 locations).

Fast forward a few years and I had actually started multiple new businesses with another co-founder, Bona. We started (and failed) a fashion technology business, we had built an eCommerce business and had grown an agency business.

So, when Bona and I first started coaching, we focused on eCommerce business owners because that was where the bulk of our experience was.

And let's just say that a LOT of the types of people you might find doing agency work or coaching in the eCommerce space are what we might call "bro marketers". You know, the ones with the flashy cars, yacht parties and private jets?

Even though I wasn't that person, this was what I saw and knew, and therefore thought I needed to be.

Which meant that I was always chasing…

I was always chasing *more*. More knowledge, more money, more of what I thought was missing.

But 12 months into it, even though we had built a multiple 6-figure coaching business, I started feeling a little bit unsatisfied, a little bit anxious, a little bit unfulfilled, a little bit misaligned… to be honest, a little bit unhappy.

That was when I attended an event held by one of my mentors, Russell Brunson called Funnel Hacking Live. There I was, on day 1, day 2, day 3 surrounded by a couple thousand other people and listening to these amazing speakers talk about their journeys and the amazing success they've had and how they love what they're doing and I just…

Felt like…

I didn't know what I was doing there.

And then on the last day, Tony Robbins spoke. He started talking about patterns of focus and how we can essentially decide to be happy, feel confident, and be who we want to be through our patterns of focus.

And it was in that moment that I had my epiphany.

He literally said one thing that changed my view on everything that I was doing completely. All he said was that we need to focus on what we *have*, not what was *missing*.

Remember when I said all I seemed to be chasing was *more*? More of what was missing?

I couldn't believe it! All this time, I was constantly just trying to fill the gaps that I perceived I was missing in myself. Knowledge, resources, the image.

And I was putting this pressure on myself to be keeping up with *everything* - the full breadth and depth of as much as possible. So much so that I was burning out.

But when he said focus on what you have? It finally gave me permission. The permission to look into my heart and find who it is I really am.

And something I am and have is that I'm an introvert that despite struggling with it all my life, has still been able to find success.

For example, in University, class participation made up 10% of my law degree marks. And I still graduated with honors. In my corporate career, I was promoted and asked to lead teams, even though I was never the loud one, the one who spoke up in meetings. I was even able to build successful 6 & 7-figure businesses even though I HATED the thought of promoting us or myself.

That's pretty remarkable, right?

And what I have is actually a gift. It's a gift that I'm an introvert that has managed to still muddle my way through being able to get promotions in my banking career, being able to muddle my way through building brands, being able to muddle my way through getting over myself…

And therefore, being able to do things like this - share my stories like this - which I can tell you even a year ago, I would not have been able to. I would not have been able to show up and connect with you like this because I was not truly being heart-centered.

And this second principle - being heart-centered - comes down to being able to share your stories from a place of vulnerability and authenticity.

Remember when I said stories were the second way we make sense of our lives? This is because stories are how we build true connection and empathy with each other. It is the honey-like lubrication we need to build relationships and know, like and trust with others.

When we are watching a love story unfold on our television screens, we can't help but think of our own love story. When we read about friendship breakups, we can't help but relive the pain of our own. When we listen to someone else's failure story, we can't help but think about the uncertainty we've experienced with our own businesses.

Stories from a heart-centered place is how we build true connection with our audience. These shared moments are how bonds form and have your buyer like and trust you so much that they can't help but want to give you their money. And not just give you their money, but share about you with other people, just like Nic did with The Choc Pot. That all comes down to your stories!

And yet, I know there are some of you reading this who might not think you have any stories to share, or you don't think you have any remarkable stories, or you might think you're just a "nobody" and who would want to listen to you anyway?

Hang with me, keep reading this book and I will share with you how it is you can find your remarkability and share your stories. Because we are ALL remarkable - each and every one of us.

But… of course, this would not be a marketing book for entrepreneurs without talking about conversions. And not just *any* type of conversions, but *rapid* conversion.

… To Rapidly Converting Followers into Buyers…

I remember looking up at our priority board and seeing the endless number of post-it notes. Bona and I have a system around creating Post-Its for every new project we want to implement. And looking at the board, I knew there was no way we would be able to implement all of this (or it would take us at least 5 years with nothing else added to it to do so!)

The alarming thing about it was that these projects were *only focused* on sales and marketing too. Things we needed to do across different platforms, different strategies and different funnels. It didn't even consider fulfillment!

I knew I needed to step away, otherwise the panic and overwhelm would grip me into inaction.

"How in the world were we going to ever do this?" was what my anxious mind was saying over and over again.

But deep down, I was also wondering whether I even wanted to. Honestly, I didn't want to be the one finding and reaching out to my potential collaboration partners. I didn't want to be the one editing my YouTube videos and optimizing the key words. I didn't want to be the one editing reels and finding the best hashtags. I didn't want to be the one actively bringing leads into my funnel.

I felt guilty because as an entrepreneur it shouldn't matter what you *want* to do, because you really should be doing it anyway! That's what being Chief Everything Officer entailed.

Not only did I realistically not have the time, but the knowledge that I was procrastinating on doing all of these very necessary activities to grow my business was draining my energy.

Call it fate, call it a higher being, call it the universe doing its thing - but that very same day I got a direct message on Facebook. It was from someone called Grace who was offering virtual assistant (VA) services. I had always played with the idea of getting a VA in the business but honestly, I hadn't known where to start to find one.

We brought her in and within weeks had completely systemized and delegated everything we wanted to do on Instagram. And not only did we not have to do the activities - but we were getting leads and making sales from it!

And then Grace introduced us to a couple of her other friends, Karen and Cyrine who were looking for work, and so we started systemizing and delegating YouTube, TikTok, Facebook, Collaboration Outreach…

And each time we were able to do this, it created more time, more energy, more leads and more sales.

We know by now that we need to create focus. The data will help us with that. We know we need to create connections between the data, our actions and our audience. The stories - behind and in front of the data - will help us with that.

Because the third principle - the last piece - is all about creating time and energy *while also creating more conversions quickly*!

Do you want to beat that sheer exhaustion I've already spoken about? And still have a growing, viable and sustainable business?

If "yes", then you need to protect your time and energy.

It wasn't until very recently that I realized just how important this third principle was. Intuitively, I knew that conversion was important (of course!), but not about the underlying principle that supports the rapidity of it, and almost on autopilot.

Not about how this is literally the only way you can do all the things you *know* you need to do in order to build your credibility and authority, reach your audience, generate leads and convert them.

Not about how this is truly the secret to me not giving into my own BS and all the excuses I was making about not doing certain things.

It all comes down to **systems**.

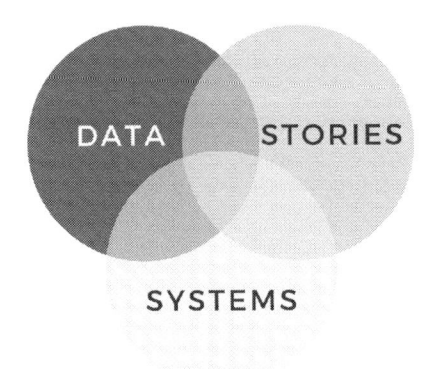

DATA   STORIES

SYSTEMS

Systems are the secret to you - as an intelligent entrepreneur - being able to rapidly and sustainably *do it all* to bank your conversions.

As your business grows, you're going to have more data points, you're going to have more stories - and opportunities to share those stories. Which means that you need to start to lift yourself from the weeds.

Do you want to be on all the different platforms? Instagram, TikTok, Facebook, Pinterest, YouTube, Podcasting, etc.?

Systems.

Do you want to be able to leverage all these different platforms in the right way to have them working for you, instead of mindlessly posting blindly so you can feel like you've at least done something?

Systems.

Do you want to be able to generate *qualified leads* every time you have a conversion event without having to agonize over where they're going to come from?

Systems!

Systems are how you create your rapid conversion machine, and be able to run it on autopilot and keep getting more sales!

You need to create systems around literally everything you do because once you can create the systems, you can delegate those systems, right? Which means more time to focus on your next horizon of data points - whether that's on a new funnel, a new product or a new platform. And more time to focus on the stories behind these data points and the stories in front to make more sales! Then you systemize and delegate those, and so on.

One of my primary goals in life is to help build the next generation of Sloth Bosses; CEOs who are intelligently lazy. CEOs who know that they want more from their business and lives than to be shackled to the "hustle". CEOs who know that while they are remarkable, they are not invincible. And that their time and energy are their most precious resources that they need to protect. And not only protect it, but still grow and lead a thriving business.

Doing all of this comes down to the third principle of Honey Trap Marketing - systems. So, if this is you - if you are our next Sloth Boss - then you are exactly in the right place!

I have now covered the *what* of Honey Trap Marketing. What it is and what the fundamental pillars are. These are your guiding principles so if you ever feel lost and unsure of what you need to do or focus on - come back to these three pillars. Data, Stories, Systems.

You will see these principles appear time and again in the rest of this book, as we go through the *how*. Because now that you know the *what*, it's time to dive into the *how*. How can you implement *Honey Trap Marketing* and know that at each stage you are balancing the data and the stories, the art and the science?

That comes down to *The Honey Trap Formula*.

2.
THE HONEY TRAP FORMULA

When I started law school, everything seemed hard. Not to humblebrag (because I think we'd just call this a brag), but I'm a pretty smart cookie. And yet, nothing was making sense!

In my first year of learning Torts and Foundations of Law, we were asked to read dozens and dozens of pages of theory and case precedent. We would then discuss what we were reading in class. And while in isolation, each class made sense, I just could not piece it all together. It just did not make sense to me.

Suffice to say that my results that first year was a blight on my academic transcript.

I entered second year with trepidation because if I couldn't even figure out the easier stuff, how in the world was I going to figure out the more advanced stuff?

I was sitting in my first class of Criminal Law when my lecturer told us that what we would be learning was just a formula - almost a cheat sheet - and that as we came across "cases" to present arguments for, we just had to go through the formula. Step by step.

And it was at that moment that everything clicked into place for me. It all started making sense. Have a murder case? Let's first go through the *actus reus* - the act, the death, the causation and the circumstances. The prosecution has to be able to prove all of these elements. And then we get into the *mens rea* - was there a reckless indifference to human life? An intent to kill? An intent to cause grievous bodily harm? Did it fall into any of the exceptions? The prosecution has to only prove one of these.

Is prosecuting or defending a murder case actually this simple? Of course not. Law cannot be boiled down to just three sentences. However, with this formula, I had the roadmap. I had the path. All I had to do was follow it, and if I went off course because I had to get into the complexities of each component (or I was distracted by something else), I knew how to get back to keep going due north.

I received my first high distinction in a law subject because I *just followed the formula*. And since then, law became so much simpler that I graduated with Honors.

Once I knew that this was what I needed in order to sustainably replicate results again and again, I started creating formulas for everything. Which is probably why it will be no surprise to you that as we get into *how* of implementing Honey Trap Marketing, it all boils down to a simple formula.

A formula that will guide you due north. And you know that if you ever find yourself getting off track, this is the path that you need to find your way back to. This formula.

$$\$\$ = M + C + T + L$$

This is simply Sales (as defined by you) being the sum of your Message, your Content, your Traffic and your Lead Attracting Conversion Event.

This is literally the path I follow each and every day to ensure we are doing and continue to do everything that we need in order to:

- Build my credibility and authority

- Create visibility and reach

- Generate qualified leads
- Convert into sales

As a bonus, for all my Sloth Bosses (👀 looking at you) - for all of you intelligent entrepreneurs leveling up to become a CEO because you know you no longer want to give into your BS - I will also be sharing with you how you can do *all of this* while only spending 2 hours a week on social media.

And that comes down to Systemization and Delegation:

$$\$\$ = \frac{M + C + T + L}{S + D}$$

The principles of *Honey Trap Marketing* - data, stories, systems - are baked into this formula. And as I go through each variable in the following chapters, you will see how integral these three principles are at each stage.

Since the technology and media landscape change so frequently, I'm making these concepts as evergreen as possible. I will be talking predominantly about strategy, frameworks, and models that you can use regardless of changes to social media. I guarantee that if you become obsessed with the formula and not the platform, you will not only be armed with what you need to implement, but also how to continue making intelligent decisions going forward.

Let's now dive into the first variable of The Honey Trap Formula: Messaging.

3.
CUTTING-THROUGH WITH YOUR MESSAGING

When there is something that may be going wrong with a situation, sometimes you'll know immediately and sometimes it just creeps up on you. Little by little.

That's what happened with our first coaching business. We were doing great, on a roll with bringing new clients in. And then… it slowly started to unravel.

We had a couple of clients here start to default on their payments. We had other clients there who were demanding immediate results without actually doing any work. I had some tough client discussions because they were blaming everything and everyone else but themselves.

No matter how many times I wanted to shake them out of it because I knew they could get results if they *just did it*, no matter how frustrated I got - to the point where I just wanted to do it for them - I knew that ultimately, they were not in it for the long haul.

And even though my whole strategy is about being heart-centered and showing up for your audience. They unfortunately just weren't.

It got to the point where I dreaded seeing client meetings and calls in the calendar.

The part that *really* bothered me was that it was becoming a pattern. It was becoming more the norm across our clients than the exception.

It was so tempting to blame them (and well… I'm not perfect so that definitely did happen for a little while), but I could not hide from the data. The data was telling me there was a pattern emerging, that this did not seem random. The stories behind the data were telling me that the pattern could only stem from one source. That common denominator? Me.

However, I knew that wasn't the *full* story behind the data because a lot of it still didn't make sense to me. What was I doing that was attracting these types of people?

Because in my mind, I wanted clients who were just like me. Willing to invest in themselves, ready to do the work, takes radical responsibility and is an action-taker. I already knew that I *am* my dreamiest buyer.

And this is the first step to cutting-through with your messaging: you have to become your dreamiest buyer.

If you're the type of person who doesn't invest in themselves then how do you expect people to invest in you? If you're the type of person who is always looking for a bargain, looking to never pay full price, then how do you expect people to pay full price for what you sell?

If you are not your own dreamiest buyer, then this will all subconsciously come out in your messaging.

In my case, I already knew that I was my own dreamiest buyer. So, what was missing?

I turned to my mentors and their experiences. The first comforting thing was that *all of them* had gone through a similar experience. It almost seemed like a coaching rite of passage to go through a phase of working with the wrong clients before finding the right ones.

And perhaps that's not surprising given that we usually start out not having found our voices yet and not having grown from experiences we *have* to have first to get the clarity on who and how we're serving.

At the time, I was modeling a lot of my messages around what seemed to resonate with more people. Remember those "bro marketers"? A lot of their messages were around ease, shortcuts and immediate *huge* results. That's what I thought worked and therefore what I needed to sell.

But when I looked more closely at how my mentors were positioning and messaging their offers, it wasn't around ease, shortcuts and immediate huge results. It was around sustainable growth with hard work. Being up front about the realities of entrepreneurship is what attracted me to them, so why did I think I needed to hide that to attract my dreamiest buyers?

It wasn't as sexy, but sexy didn't matter any longer. I wanted clients who would come in with eyes wide open and who would actually do the work to get results.

Now I may have mentioned that the wrong clients were the norm rather than the exception, but I should also add that I had some AMAZING clients - clients who were my dreamiest buyers (you'll be reading more about them and their stories in this book). So at least I knew I wasn't *completely* off-base. I just needed to tweak some things to get more of them!

So, I did what I do best - I learnt from them. I learnt who they were, how they thought and what attracted them to me. And it inspired me to let go of any insecurities and doubts I had about needing to be someone different with my messaging.

Once I did that; once I not only became my dreamiest buyer, but aligned *all* of my messaging to that person - then I started getting meaningful cut-through and I started serving clients who were willing to pay, who showed up for themselves, who didn't make excuses, who put in the work and ultimately got the results.

So, this is our starting point. Our starting point is to become the buyer we want to attract and create messages from that place. Aligned with who we are (not someone we *think* we need to be). This is the mindset shift you *must* make in order to get cut-through with your messaging.

Let's now get into the tangible steps of creating and testing your messages.

What's Their Before and After?

Our aspirations, desires, and wants are (almost) always based in the future. We're *here* now. We're going *there*. When we get *there*, our desires are fulfilled. We feel comfort, security, alleviation of pain, and happiness. It's this connection to a future outcome that creates an internal imperative to purchase something.

Think about it for a minute. Why did you buy this book? There are specific reasons you could report. At a superficial level, "I want more leads" may be one. Yet, if we dig a little deeper, there's more to it than just getting leads. Getting more leads is connected to earning money, and less frustration. It's also connected to a sense of achievement, and *certainty* that you're doing the right thing, and not the wrong thing. When it comes to getting more leads, you have your own desire that is unique to you. It's the story you tell yourself (subconsciously) about why getting this book was a good choice. That subconscious process is what we call *mapping out the before and after*.

Mapping the before and after gives you the ability to help your buyers envision the life-changing after-effects of your products and services. Not only will they embrace those positive qualities of that future result, they'll also feel a tremendous sense of internal tension between that desire and the mediocrity or pain of life before. That's when your products and offers sell like crazy. That's when your buyer lands on your site or sales page, not just thinking about the features or price, but fantasizing and craving what their life is going to look, feel, and sound like when they experience the after effects.

It could be a cooling face wash after a hot summer day and feeling refreshed, relaxed, and ready for a social gathering. It could be the sense of connectedness, acceptance, and love they now feel from going through your relationship program. Make them go starry eyed and show them by painting a picture in their minds!

In the lead up to one of our Challenges, one of the first exercises I walk our participants through is helping them determine whether their offer or product is a "painkiller" or a "vitamin." I ask our participants: "Is your offer positioned to help your customer move away from pain, or move toward pleasure?"

At the core of human motivation, we have two basic patterns. The first is that we move away from pain. The second is that we move toward pleasure. If you want people to buy your products or services, you'll need to determine what the primary driver is for your customer and talk to that effectively in your marketing.

Think about this with something basic: taxes. If you don't file your taxes by x date, you're going to suffer a penalty. If you don't know how to file your taxes properly, you're going to spend more money than you need to. You'll also waste a ton of time. These three facts are what drive accounting firms' sales, QuickBooks, and other accounting software. Those services and products help you stay organized and therefore: out of trouble (painkiller).

People don't buy skincare, nutrition, or workout products because they love *possessing* them. That psychological need for acceptance is running in the background at all times. We want to look good. Why? Because we want to be accepted by our peers. Why? Because we're afraid of not being loved and accepted. We're afraid of being left out or worse: *left behind*. A core desire for humans is validation and status. Hence people go through extraordinary measures to fit in and be "good enough" to avoid the pain of exclusion, which is oftentimes attached to our materiality. These products, then, are painkillers.

I would hazard a guess that *all* coaching, consultants and service providers have a painkiller offer. Even if you might think yours is not, I would delve deeper to get to the actual root cause - the need - for what you do. For example, helping people lose weight isn't just about looking good, and not even about feeling good - it's about being able to be on this earth for a long time to play with children and grandchildren, to be able to grow old with partners and loved ones, to be able to fulfill potential to the fullest. Having a painkiller offer is a good thing, because when you can talk to that pain it immediately makes you an authority on the subject.

Painkillers relieve pain. Vitamin products add something to our lives. What type of product do you have? Are you helping someone move away from a problem they have in their lives, or are you helping them move towards an aspiration, a goal? Make a bullet point list of the symptoms and different ways they manifest. How does it affect your buyers' relationships, money, satisfaction, self-esteem, or time? What are they thinking, feeling, saying or doing right now, before they've received your product or service, when they've received your product or service, while they're using it and finally when they get the result that they are after?

In fashion and accessories, not having the right outfit could inhibit Mary's ability to speak to her boss confidently. It might make her feel self-conscious among her colleagues. What's life currently like now? And then speak into the positive future. Continuing Mary's example: it's that moment when Mary walks into the room, and someone notices her. She's walking through the doorway into the office, or the online meeting, and her coworker gives her a compliment. It's the moment when she can stride (not walk) into a meeting with her boss, it's the moment at which she notices that she's smiling at herself more frequently in the bathroom mirror (vitamin).

One of my previous clients, Christine, sells dog bows and bandanas. She used to struggle with thinking through the result she's trying to get her customer. "I just sell dog bows", she used to say. But she doesn't just sell dog bows. She sells the fact that dogs deserve to feel confident too.

We're not consciously making these assessments. We're never like, "Oh, I want this product or service because I really want some external validation, or because I want to avoid being mocked and laughed at." All those feelings happen beneath the surface of our consciousness. We never know consciously what the underlying root-cause is... we only ever think or feel the symptoms.

Think like a doctor. As a doctor, when someone walks into your office, they say, "I have a headache. I'm dizzy and tired. I can't sleep." You hear what they're saying, and you understand those are symptoms. Those symptoms are top of mind. Those symptoms they're feeling - before they've tried your painkiller or vitamin offer - are how you will talk about your customer's Before point.

What Symptoms Are They Feeling?

When you empathize and speak to someone about their symptoms – almost better than they can in their own words – you build immediate trust and rapport, which is why it's such an effective marketing tool. However, how do you go from empathizing with their symptoms to getting them to buy your product or service? The answer is to move them through the stages of the buying decision-making process: being symptom-aware, to problem-aware, to solution-aware.

SYMPTOM-AWARE → **PROBLEM-AWARE** → **SOLUTION-AWARE**

I asked you to think like a doctor in the previous section. When someone comes into your office and says "I have a headache. I'm dizzy and tired. I can't sleep", they are relaying their symptoms. Here, they are symptom-aware. They are aware of the things that they are thinking, feeling and doing at their Before point.

They are not yet problem-aware, until you, as the doctor, diagnose them. Perhaps the cause of their symptoms – the "problem" - is that they have a brain tumor (not to be extreme or anything) This is the reason they are feeling those symptoms. Once you have diagnosed them, they become problem-aware. They know now what is causing the pain they have been feeling.

Once they know what their problem is, they're going to want to fix it! And this is when they become solution-aware. They will want the painkiller or the vitamin you're offering because it is going to help them relieve the symptoms they've been feeling, and remove the cause of their problem. This is how we go from talking to someone's symptoms, building that trust and rapport with them, to having them buy our product, and get them to their After point.

For anyone with a vitamin product, where you are moving someone towards pleasure, you might be reading this getting stuck on the word "problem". Because you might think you don't help solve a problem. And this is when I would encourage you to go back to the symptoms. At the point in time when they realize they need to buy your product, what are they thinking, saying, feeling and doing? If you sell indoor plants, is it that they are feeling the emptiness and lack of life inside a room or an apartment? If you sell scrunchies and hair bows, is it because they wanted to feel a connection with their daughter through doing her hair with something pretty?

One of my clients, Anu, is a curator of beautiful South-East Asian art. Her customers currently feel uninspired by their surroundings and want to create an environment that is uplifting, calming and striking all at the same time.

We are all feeling something when we make a purchase. There is always a reason behind it. You might just need to dig a little deeper to find yours.

Because once you can empathize with the symptoms your ideal customers are feeling, then moving them to buy through your marketing messages becomes infinitely simpler.

To move them to buy, we need to start tapping into their emotions. And to do this, we need to "paint the picture."

How Do You Paint the Picture?

A few years before we made the move to New York City, Ash and I came to visit for a holiday in the spring. It was the second time we had been to NYC and it was a different experience because we had gotten the "touristy stuff" out of our system already.

This time, we found a small place in Chelsea to stay. We experienced the city as a local. We found an amazing bagel breakfast spot (the café on 22nd Ash couldn't stay away from). We had our afternoon walk routes on the Highline and the Greenway. We experienced all sorts of New York magic.

We were on one of our walks back from the Greenway, on a nondescript street. It was my favorite time in the twilight hours of that spring evening. The sun was close to setting and the sky was turning into a beautiful pinkish-orange color. People started turning on their lights in their houses, families were starting to settle down for the night together, and there was optimism, love, and beauty in the air. Then, Ash turned to me and asked me something that I believe changed the trajectory of our lives. He said "could you imagine living here and these were our evenings?"

With that one question, I knew this was where I was meant to be at some point. He managed to take everything we were hearing, seeing and feeling, and boil it down to one question that vividly painted the picture for me. And from that, I was swept away. The vision was in my mind and I couldn't let it go. And a few short years later, we made the move.

I've always been fascinated with what makes people buy. This is the stuff I geek out about. And after having gone through that experience myself, I know how powerful it is to paint the picture for someone.

Your customers must envision themselves getting a result from your solutions (literally, a subconscious vision). So, as much as you can, paint a picture for them. Use your stories, language and imagery that shakes them out of their "conserve energy, stay in comfort mode," and compels them to get the benefits you're offering from your products or services.

What does the "promised land" look like for them? What transformation can you help them achieve by relieving their symptoms and helping them solve their problem (or reach their aspiration) with your offer.

If you can do this, you are making it so much easier for them to make the mental leap to just buy because you are starting to tap into their *emotions*, the primary driver for all our decision-making. Your potential buyers need to know that they don't have to be someone else, be somewhere else, to achieve what they want to. They don't have to fundamentally change who they are in order to get to that "After" point you are promising them. You're already starting to lower the automatic barriers they put up to resist buying.

A great example of this is saranoni.com. They sell blankets. But blankets are a means to an end. That end isn't "keep your body warm." It's the future vision of a cuddle party with your son or daughter. It's a Sunday, connecting with your family. The people at Saranoni.com are absolutely brilliant at painting pictures like that, and selling their vitamin product.

One of our clients, Edward of UpLevel Entrepreneur, helps 6-figure CEOs untangle the mess of their finances, bank accounts and taxes so that they not only feel in control, but they feel smart about scaling into the $1m club and *actually make money*. He paints the picture of a successful CEO making intelligent boss moves, and therefore being able to take his family on ski trips, play golf, own a boat, simply by making the complex simple.

If you want to start to distill these concepts I've spoken about into messages for your audience, how would you go about it? Here's an exercise that will help:

1. In paragraph form, write what a day FEELS like in your dreamiest buyer's life. The purpose of this is building as much empathy as possible with this person. If you've already made the mindset shift I spoke about at the beginning of this chapter, you wouldn't even need to imagine it. Because you will already have *become* your dreamiest buyer.
2. On a single sheet of paper, write "Moving toward" and "Moving away from   "
3. Place a line between the two.
4. List as many symptoms as you can in the "Moving away from" column.
5. Start painting the picture in the "Moving toward" column - vividly describe what their "promised land" or transformation will be (what it would look, sound and feel like) with your offer.

Messaging always starts with the stories. The stories that are derived from bringing the symptoms to life at your dreamiest buyer's Before point, and by painting the picture of their After point.

These stories provide a rich starting point for us. It helps us capture the essence and theme of what we'd like to say and talk about in our messages. But what about the actual words? How do we come up with one (max two) sentences that not only encapsulates what we're trying to convey, but also captures the attention of our audience?

This is where Message Hacking comes in.

Message Hacking

Message Hacking are practical ways for you to form your thoughts around your buyer's Before & After into *their* words. This is a powerful way for you to connect with your audience and have them thinking "get out of my head!"

Depending on your product or service, there are multiple ways you can hack messages at the time of writing this book. By the time you read it, given the proliferation of new technologies and platforms, there may be even *more* ways. Ultimately, you want to find places where your dreamiest buyers are already conversing or giving feedback.

For example, shopping platforms like Amazon, eBay and Etsy are the best places for a product-based business to see the words their buyers use. Find competitor products and scour the reviews their customers have left for them. What are the actual words they're using to describe the product type in general, and then the specific product they're talking about? How can you use anything negative they're saying as "symptoms" in your messaging? How can you use anything positive they're saying to "paint the picture" in your own messaging?

If you have a service-based or coaching business, you could try looking at platforms like Reddit or other message boards. Facebook, especially within Groups, are a great place to see what buyers of services and coaching programs are saying.

You just want to be making sure that the problems, the symptoms you are seeing are aligned to *your* dreamiest buyer. Not all businesses will find their dreamiest buyers on these platforms. If this is the case, then the best way to message hack is to *talk* to your dreamiest buyers. Especially if you already have some as clients. Have a really good conversation with them and note the actual words they are saying. How are they describing their problems? Why did they decide to start working with you? What are they loving about working with you? What improvements and results are they already seeing and experiencing?

One of our clients, Dawn, runs a coaching program helping people earn an income and move to an overseas paradise. She message hacks extremely well by asking her audience through one of her Facebook Group admission questions. As a result, she's been able to create messages that not only talk to her dreamiest buyer's Before & After, but do it in their words! Messages like:

1. I'd consider moving overseas if I only knew where to start…
2. If I had the income to live anywhere, I'd move abroad
3. You can create a dream life overseas. How to retire in paradise on a shoestring budget
4. True or False? I want to move overseas I just don't know where
5. If I'm going to retire in paradise, I want to have a plan
6. Living the Dream 🌴 Without Worrying About $$$
7. An Overseas Location… check. Necessary Income… check. A Plan to Make it Happen… NOPE.
8. Want a step-by-step roadmap to live the overseas life you have imagined?
9. It is Time to Go? Best decision ever to leave the USA and live in Mexico
10. True or False? You want an affordable alternative to escape the USA
11. Do you agree? The only thing to stop me from living overseas is earning income

Dawn's messages are extremely powerful at getting right to the heart of her dreamiest buyer's biggest concerns and aspirations.

Another client, Michelle, used message hacking for her boutique for mothers. She was at her son's soccer practice and had her dreamiest buyers on the sidelines with her. What better time to do a little message hacking?

Out of her conversations, Michelle gained some amazing message ideas. Things like:

1. How to make a "cool mom": 1. Venti coffee 2. Heavy dose of sarcasm 3. Some great boutique clothes
2. I just want to be mistaken for the nanny at my kid's soccer practice. Are there clothes for that?
3. Show me stylish clothes that don't require a "bounce back" after pregnancy
4. Moms want a personal stylist who can plan easy but stylish looks on a mat leave budget
5. True or false? "Mom" clothes can be comfortable and stylish
6. Help! Some days I can barely keep the kids alive. I definitely don't have time to put together a cute outfit
7. I need jeans that "move with me" because I'm always carrying three bags and chasing a toddler
8. #momstyle Confidence is your best accessory. A Starbucks is the second-best accessory
9. Boutique clothes. Designed for moms. Easy styling guides

Do you see the power of using the words your dreamiest buyers are actually *using* to bring to life your Before & After? THIS is how you start to tell stories *in front* of the data and strongly connect with them so they are thinking of you the next time they feel those symptoms.

Another great way to Message Hack is to use tools like the Google auto-complete feature, answerthepublic.com and answersocrates.com to see what types of questions people are asking on the internet. When using the Google auto-complete feature, start typing in your topic in the search bar and you will see Google predict the rest of your search based on commonly asked questions. Answer the Public and Answer Socrates operate similarly, where you put in your keyword and they will surface questions being searched on the internet. These tactics will give you some really great messages to test with your audience!

At this point, you might have brainstormed a *whole* bunch of messages, and now you're not exactly sure which angle to go down. What will *actually* resonate with your audience? What will cut-through all the noise? What will get your dreamiest buyers to move to the next step with you?

This is when we use the data.

How Can You Use Data to Determine Your Winning Messages?

Before getting into business, I didn't quite understand the importance of marketing. It sounds silly to admit that now, but there you go. I had operated under the (mistaken) assumption that as long as you had a great product or service and a passion for providing it, our doors would be flooded.

This may be true for some business owners - I have come across a few who have built their business purely on referrals. However, having spoken to them, I also know these business owners had put plenty of time and effort into creating connections and networks to be able to tap into. And even now, these referral networks are drying up. Which puts an even greater importance on marketing.

Because I didn't quite understand the importance of marketing, I didn't quite understand the importance of messaging. I used to create titles that just went straight to the point of what the content was about. I didn't realize these needed to be written as "hooks" that would create curiosity in my ideal buyer. I didn't consider symptoms; I didn't consider painting the picture. I didn't consider anything close to Message Hacking. My logical brain just went straight to telling my audience what I was going to talk about.

It's probably no surprise to know that the show-up rate at that time was woefully low. After having discovered the art of messaging, there was something still bothering me. I had so many different angles that I could go down. For example, did my current audience care the most about building credibility and authority? Did they care more about getting reach and visibility? Or was it mostly about generating leads? Or was it all about saving time?

While I knew I could test different messages by changing the hook for a conversion event (e.g., my webinar) and running traffic there for a period of time to assess conversion rates, testing like this would take a lot of time and money.

There had to be a quicker, simpler and cheaper way.

That was when we came across a sprint-testing methodology we learnt from Jessica Jobes. While her focus was mainly on how this can improve advertising conversions, we saw what she was doing and knew this should be able to work to test *just* our messaging as well. And so, we tested it.

We tested it with all of *my* businesses and saw phenomenal results. We tested it with all of our clients' businesses and similarly saw phenomenal results.

We saw time and time again that the messages we *thought* would resonate with our audience, actually *didn't*. Because we now had data from a statistically significant number of people from an objective audience - still comprised of our target buyers - that we could point to, rather than trying to just rely on our own opinion on what we think will cut-through to our audience.

Let's play a little game amongst ourselves. We're going to take Dawn's messages as an example. Read through the eleven messages she tested and pick your favorite - the one you think won. Go back to page 33 and do that now.

Have you done it? Picked your favorite? The message you think that her dreamiest buyers would most resonate with?

After spending only $21 on ads over a couple of days, three of her messages performed really well:

4. True or False? I want to move overseas I just don't know where

10. True or False? You want an affordable alternative to escape the USA

11. Do you agree? The only thing to stop me from living overseas is earning income

Were any of these the ones you picked? I can tell you that they weren't on the top of my list! Which may not be too much of a surprise because I am not in Dawn's target audience.

This is why when any of my clients ask me for my opinion, I point them to the data instead. How do we get the learnings and results we need using data from your dreamiest buyers?

Through a data-driven test I call **Messagelytics**.

Would you like to know how to run this incredibly cost-effective and quick test?

Yes? Well then, let's get into it!

Running Your Messagelytics Test

By now, you should have a whole list of messages brainstormed and written down. What we're going to do is pick around ten of them to test.

And we're going to create color-blocked graphics with them. Color-blocking is when you take contrasting colors and put them next to each other to create something eye-catching. This is the purpose of color-blocking - we are looking to "stop the scroll".

A client of ours, Dyonne, ran a Messagelytics test for her business Other Venue - a 2-sided unique venue booking platform. She created this business when she identified the need for an easier way to book a unique venue while planning her wedding.

Dyonne already had a hypothesis of her client's Before & After points, but message hacked it by speaking directly to venue owners. Owners of places like art galleries and farms.

Here is an example of one round of her color-block graphic tests:

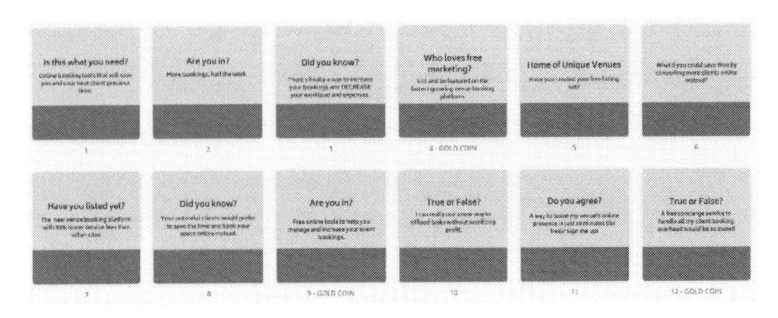

Dyonne used the contrasting colors of yellow against purple. You will notice that there is nothing else on these graphics - just the colors and the words. No logo, no other images. The purpose of this test is to "ask" your audience which message they resonate the most with.

It doesn't matter what colors you use, as long as they are bright and contrast with each other and that the text is readable.

At the time of writing this, running a traffic campaign optimized for link clicks on Facebook is the most effective way to run Messagelytics. The purpose of this campaign is NOT to make any sales, conversions, registrations. Rather, it is a quick, easy and cheap way to ask *your* audience on Facebook to take an action based purely on the words on the graphic - to click the link.

You want to be looking out for any messages that are getting under 80c a click (the threshold at the time of writing this book). These messages are your winners for the round.

Now that you know what messages actually resonate with your audience based on data, what do you do with them?

What to Do with Your Winning Messages

Great news! You know the messages that will cut-through to your audience, what the heck should we now do with them?

In short, you want to use them *everywhere*.

You want to use them everywhere so that you can become known for what you do!

There are two levels I think about using my winning messages: 1) as hooks; and 2) as content themes.

Let's discuss hooks first. Hooks are the words you use to create curiosity and compel someone to care about what it is you're telling them. For example, a hook on a webinar registration page is designed to compel a person to continue down the page to learn more about what the webinar is about. A hook on an ad is designed to compel a person to want to click through the ad to learn more. A hook on a caption is designed to compel a person to want to click "see more" to read what else you have to say.

Hooks are how you grab your dreamiest buyer's attention and entice them to keep going on the journey with you. If we don't get our hooks right, we don't have a hope of growing our audience, generating leads and ultimately making sales.

It reminds me of the time we got our kitten, Puffington. If you've been following me on any of my social media accounts, you would know I have an adorably stand-offish British Shorthair cat. He wants nothing to do with me most of the day except for perhaps a 10-minute window in the day when *he* feels like some company.

When Ash and I decided to get a kitten, we found a breeder in Sydney who had a litter that was around 4 weeks old. We drove the 45 minutes it took for us to get there so that we could have a look at these kittens and see if there was one for us.

Now of course, we fell in love with all six or seven who were in the litter. I'm only human after all! Our issue, however, was how in the world we were going to choose the ONE for us, when all of them were equally gorgeous. When the breeder asked us which one we wanted so he could tag it, I honestly didn't know!

I started thinking. "You know what… they're super cute, but we can wait a bit. It doesn't have to be now."

Who else stalls on a decision like this when they're feeling a little overwhelmed? When there is nothing there that is compelling enough to make it stand out?

There we were standing in front of a litter of kittens, unable to make a decision, take action, progress to the next step, and therefore about to leave, when suddenly! We saw the cage door - which was meant to be locked and clearly wasn't - burst open and this little ball of fur with teeny little legs scurrying out across the floor.

This 4-week-old kitten had head-butted the door open himself and we knew - then and there - that this little cheeky one was meant to be part of our family.

Now what does this story have to do with creating hooks? Because if you want to create an effective hook, it has to pattern interrupt!

As you know, there is a LOT of content out there. We scroll mindlessly all the time through so much content on Facebook, Instagram, Pinterest, YouTube, our email inbox. Literally everywhere!

And what this means is that people don't stop. There is an overwhelming amount of content, a lot of it is meh or same-same. So, people won't stop. They won't read or listen to what you have to say and they'll move on... like we almost did when we couldn't choose a kitten.

Every single one of those kittens was worthy of being chosen, just like everyone's content is worthy of being read.

BUT if you want to have people stop and choose you. Like we stopped and chose Puffington, you need to interrupt or break a pattern. Which is all about changing the current momentum or direction that person is in. You need to get in front of them as they're mindlessly doing what they're doing and BREAK IT!

And for you - this means you have to think about how you hook people in with an eye-catching scroll-stopping headline.

No matter what it is you are writing copy for - it could be a social media post, an ad, a website header, a lead magnet - it needs a hook.

And one of the most effective ways of creating a hook that pattern interrupts, that compels your dreamiest buyers to keep reading what you have to say, is to use one of your winning messages. Something that you have already tested and validated through Messagelytics.

If it can be plugged straight in, then awesome, less work for you! If it needs a little massaging, go ahead and make any edits you need to have it fit in that context. At least you know now that your hook has been created off really solid starting foundations based on data, rather than just your own opinion or guesswork.

The second level in which we can use our winning messages is in our content. Your winning messages will tell you the *essence* of what it is your audience cares about. For example, Dawn's audience wants to know more about how they can afford to move overseas, where it might make sense and how they can do it while still earning and income. She has now created podcast content and a book from these messages.

Michelle's dreamiest buyers want to know more about styling guides and outfit combinations that make it easy for a busy mom to run around with her kids and still look "put together". She has now confidently created social media content based on these messages.

Another of our clients, Bimpe, sells skincare for men. A message that did really well through Messagelytics was all about razor bumps. She went live on Instagram and spoke about the 3 tips to prevent shaving bumps. It was one of the most viewed and engaged videos on her feed.

Knowing what it is your dreamiest buyers actually care about based on data is the starting point for creating your content. Let's now delve more deeply into content creation - the next variable of The Honey Trap Formula.

4.
CREATING YOUR CONTENT HONEY TRAPS

For many of us, content creation is the bane of our existence. It seems to take up way too much time for the results it provides (which is incredibly hard to track!).

However, I think we all know that it is still a necessary evil. Necessary because it ultimately helps us build our credibility and authority. Without content, no one would know what you do. Without content, no one would know the value you provide. Without content, no one would be able to come to know, like and trust you.

And spoiler alert: Without content, you would not be able to call your dreamiest buyers forward. Creating quality content *will* help you generate quality leads. I'll be going over this in the next chapter.

All of these reasons I've just stated, actually make creating content an incredibly valuable activity you should be focusing on as an entrepreneur. However, I'll call out right now that you should only be spending 1 hour tops *actually creating it* for the whole week (and I'm talking about multiple posts, reels, videos, stories and TikToks per day 😉).

I'm not talking about repurposing, I'm talking about reconceptualizing into these as much as possible, you want to be focusing on creating two types of content:

1. **Content Trust Accelerators**, that are share-worthy and engage-worthy, and has your audience coming to know, like and trust you; and

2. **Content Honey Traps**, that create so much curiosity that your audience *has* to follow you through your front-end funnel.

There should be *at least* a 50/50 split between these two types of content. Ultimately, the more that people share about you and see you, the more that they will come to trust you and open their wallets up to you.

This phenomenon comes down to something I read in Daniel Priestley's book *Oversubscribed*. He talks about a concept called the 7-Hour Rule. The 7-Hour Rule says that someone must spend at least 7 hours with your brand to buy and become a fan.

For example, 7 hours into binge watching on Stranger Things or Game of Thrones, and I can't help but rave about it to others I meet. After reading way more than seven hours of Harry Potter, I'm excited to experience the virtual reality experience, *Chaos at Hogwarts* in the NYC store (super nerdy I know!). After reading more than seven hours of Naomi Novik's Deadly Education series, I'm pre-buying the next book in the series - that I have to wait 8 months for! After 7 hours invested into each of these things, I 100% recommend them to others.

Now, why is 7 hours so important? Because any time you are selling something, you must establish trust first. If you're creating Content Trust Accelerators, which means that you are adding value to your dreamiest buyers at no cost *and* your content is being shared by others, you are building trust with your people.

Let me tell you about the time I stumbled upon how to do this.

With The Choc Pot, it was never my intention to create share-worthy content. Not really. We were just focused on creating great products and a great experience. When we first started, we didn't even know what good content even was!

You know by now that Ash had worked to perfect my all-time favorite dessert for me - a chocolate molten lava cake - the type that when you break the thin cakey-shell, it just suddenly oozes chocolate and basically covers the plate. A share-worthy product, right?

And through his tinkering with it, we created The Choc Pot - literally our namesake product.

And this is what I mean by us stumbling upon it. In a way, we were fortunate to have started our business with a pretty share-worthy product that created share-worthy content.

And once people started coming into The Choc Pot, it was inevitable. We were able to catch like wildfire because *everyone* who was coming in was sharing about us. And with this sharing, more and more people came to trust us.

Even people who never came in were sharing about us! We were reposted by Kim Kardashian's best friend at the time, Jonathan Cheban a.k.a. @foodgod.

This particular dessert carried us for a couple of years, and then like with all things, the "hype" started to die down. And this was when I became fascinated about the concept of building Content Trust Accelerators.

Because when I looked around me, I saw how pervasive the #cameraeatsfirst culture had become. I knew we had to see if we could recreate another share-worthy product and content. And so, we tried a few different things, months and months and months of creating new desserts as part of what we call our Dessert of The Month - a new dessert we launched and had on the menu for one month only.

And while some of them did ok, there wasn't anything that really stood out. Not to the level of The Choc Pot dessert.

And then...

We FINALLY found one that hit and started getting shared over and over and over again - It was the Waffnut:

And because we had such great success with it, we eventually developed a whole range of them and they became a permanent fixture on the menu.

What I had here was a formula for creating share-worthy content through our PRODUCT. I realized that the products that were share-worthy created some kind of physiological arousal. Literally, a strong attraction because of how beautiful it looked. It needed either some type of natural movement, like what you saw with The Choc Pot (i.e., the oozy molten chocolate). Or it needed height like what you saw with the Waffnut.

And I'll be going into why these are important a little later.

But for now, I also just want to be really clear that when I say "content", I don't just mean a product you have or a post you do. I actually mean content in broader terms - it could be stories you create or others create about you, it could be news, information, ideas, messages…

Anything that mentions you or can be linked back to you is what I mean by "content". Because the *power* of being shared to build trust is in the little stories and in the little moments, when people casually bring you, your brand, your product up in context of what you do. Just like Nic did when he was raving about The Choc Pot (to me)!

Now ever since, I've been trying to work out how we translate the formula I had stumbled upon in hospitality into other industries, especially with our coaching business. Because I'm going to be honest, it has not been as easy! And you can already see why… visually it's just not the same.

So, I took some learnings from authors like Jonah Berger on creating viral content, tested it with our own content for The Growth Boss (our first coaching business), as well as with our content for Capsho when we transitioned our business. We started working with some clients and their offer, we started Content Hacking (more on this later) - and through testing, learning and keeping track of the data on all of this content - we hit on a few key principles that resulted in people sharing and engaging, coming to trust us. And these principles are what make up the foundations of the Content Trust Accelerators.

I am going to first share with you the key principles to creating *Content Trust Accelerators* and then we are going to extend upon that into creating your *Content Honey Traps*.

Let's now get into the three key principles to creating Content Trust Accelerators: Emotions, Storytelling and Practical Value.

Let's start with emotions.

How Do We Tap into Our Audience's Emotions?

Have you ever been out with your friends or family and there was a moment where you felt compelled to take photos? Perhaps in your mind, you thought "this will be nice to share with my friends on social media", or even just "what a great memory". You probably had a pretty logical reason for wanting to take that photo. But underlying that very logical reason was a not so logical one - you felt something.

You felt happy or nostalgic or surprised. Perhaps you felt like this particular moment would never happen again. This *emotion* you felt was the true reason that compelled you to take the photo.

The same goes for any other action you take.

Imagine standing at the bottom of Niagara Falls. Where the power of the running water falling 170ft is so intense that even when you know you are safe on the observation deck, you are still getting wet from the mist of the Falls. As you get closer, you look up and feel the power of the Falls get stronger. You feel dizzy and step back.

You are amazed. You are humbled. You feel elevated. You feel awe.

Every time we feel an emotion, it is always accompanied by some type of physiological reaction. The heart beats faster, blood pressure rises, we pump our fists in the air, we run around the living room.

And when we feel an emotion that excites us, like awe, we can't help wanting to tell people all about it, all about what happened. That's just inherent in our nature and in our need to share.

So ultimately, you want to be thinking about how you can inspire this physiological reaction in your content.

Because emotions are what compels people to take action.

This can be brought to life in your content in a variety of ways. For example, it could be your actual product that inspires an emotion like awe, it could be an amazing experience your buyer had that is awe-inspiring for them, it could just be in the stories you share of your own experiences that induce awe.

It does not have to be some *big* gesture; it just has to be something markedly different to what people are used to - to prompt them to share about it.

For example, we had created desserts that visually inspired awe and excitement. Every time someone broke through the shell of The Choc Pot and discovered the abundance of molten chocolate underneath, they felt awe. Every time a team member delivered a Waffnut dessert to a table, the height and colors of the dessert created awe and excitement.

And with these emotions being tapped into, people took action, took photos and they shared. They shared about our desserts through content, accelerating trust.

For other businesses who may not have the benefit of a visually exciting product, they could be creating awe through their care, their customer service and their onboarding experience.

For example, a friend of mine, Jen, shared this post on Facebook, commenting about what a great experience this person, Diane, had with chewy.com. In short, Diane had received her subscription of dog food from Chewy 3 days before her dog died. She called their customer service wanting to know what her options were. They not only gave her a refund, asked her to give the food to a shelter who would need it, but *also* sent her roses and a sympathy card for her loss.

Imagine you were in Diane's shoes… how would you feel having lost a loved pet and being treated with this much love, compassion and kindness from "strangers"? It is this feeling that prompted Diane to do something, to take action. That action was simply sharing about her experience and urging others to become a customer as well.

And as you can see, just her one shared story was shared again, over 84,000 times! What better way is there to create and accelerate trust?

This is why tapping into our audience's emotions is so key to creating Content Trust Accelerators. There are *so many* ways you might be able to think about evoking emotions, and in particular, inspiring awe in your audience. Can you send a physical onboarding package that creates surprise, shock and awe? Can you create an event that surpasses their wildest expectations? Can you provide *so much value* that they can't believe they only paid $x (or even got it for free!)?

There are countless ways you can evoke emotions in your audience. List them all down and test them. What works to have people share about you and what you do? I've just taken you through the secret to having your audience share about you and starting to create trust in your content - tapping into their emotions. What else can *you* specifically do in your own content to compel people to trust you?

It comes down to two things: Storytelling and providing practical value.

How Do We Master the Art of Storytelling?

Remember that story I told you about Nic raving about The Choc Pot to James and I? The amazing thing about it is that Nic barely even mentioned our product. That whole time he was talking about The Choc Pot, he was actually recounting our story – my and Ash's story.

It got to the point where it was even a little bit creepy that he knew some of the details, until I realized that it was because we actually had a snippet of our story printed right on the front page of our menu…

AN EPIC DESSERT MENU
the choc pot

OUR STORY

Pinpointing that exact moment when you can say you're in love is hard to find. There may be those small, incremental moments that sneak up on you and builds, but I'm referring to the ones where time stand stills, everything around you seems to move in slow motion, and you realise in that exact moment that you're in love.

For me, there were two distinct moments belting out the climax to Lionel Richie's song 'Truly' together in the car, looking over and realising that you really mean it about each other, and that first dip into the dessert Ash made me, past the pudding crust and into absolutely deliciously flowing, molten chocolate.

The romance of love and passion conquering all has never been truer than in our story. We've both come from completely different backgrounds. In fact, Ash gave up studying medicine to pursue his culinary dreams. He makes fresh, home-made chocolate desserts using quality ingredients such as Callebaut chocolate, unrefined caster sugar and jersey milk, to name a few. He makes everything fresh on-site, from the soufflés and waffles to the marshmallows and salted caramel. And me? I just wanted to bring the same happiness I've enjoyed to others – in the form of deliciously fresh desserts.

Love life & live cheeky!
Ash & Deej xx

I knew (or maybe gut-knew), even from the very beginning, the stories we hear are *what stick*. It's how we as humans take in information, it's how we make sense of the world. Which is why through the ages, you'll notice that information is never passed down just as information, but instead through stories. Stories are how we make information stick.

Think about a time you were learning about something relatively boring and dry. Perhaps you were in an economics class or history class? When you try to recall anything you may have learnt, what comes to mind? I know, it may have been a while ago 😅 but let's see if we can try anyway.

When I think about history for example, do you know what I remember? I remember being fascinated with figures like William Wallace. Not because I knew his information - things like his exact date of birth and the dot points of his Wikipedia page - but because I had seen and read his *story*. It may have been sensationalized through a Mel Gibson blockbuster, but that movie, *Braveheart,* telling William Wallace's story is what brought him to life for me - enough that I cared about who he was and what he did, to the point that I ended up doing even more of my own research. The story had stuck in my mind in a way that I *wanted* to learn more information.

This is how we start to get cut-through in our content and how we talk about what we do and how we do it (i.e., the information). Through our stories. Information about your brand, offer, service, product is woven so deeply into your story's narrative that people cannot tell your story without inadvertently mentioning it. So that every time your story is shared, so are you!

In fact, one of our previous clients, Liuba shared this particular win inside our private community. Liuba sells skincare and she posted this message she received from a customer who was about to put her third big order in, and this customer actually said *"I love your story which is why I was drawn to your line".*

This is why telling your stories is *so* powerful in creating Content Trust Accelerators.

Let's take an example - the Google Parisian Love ad. If you have not seen this ad yet, you have to watch it! Google "Google Parisian Love ad" and you are sure to find it…

This story, strangely enough, is not about Google. Yet, Google is woven so deeply into the story that you cannot be blamed for thinking it might be.

The story is about an unknown person's journey to finding love and how these seemingly small, inconsequential moments in this person's life have led to big, milestone changes - all captured in his Googling history.

This ad is incredibly clever in so many ways. One I've already mentioned: because the brand and product itself is woven in so seamlessly, that it is barely even there. Even though it's all we see.

The other is because it creates such a deep connection with us, the audience. When we watched the story unfold - this love story - we cannot help but think of our own love stories.

We all probably know by now that our lives are always centered around ourselves. It's nothing to be ashamed of and is completely understandable. The only mind we know is our own. The only thoughts we know are our own. The only perspectives we know are our own. The only lives we've fully experienced are our own. Which is why every time we read or watch another story; we actually consume it within our own frames. We watch or read other people's stories and we bring *our own* set of thoughts, experiences and perspectives to it. We just can't help it. And this is also exactly why stories are so powerful in creating connections.

Every time you watch a heartbreaking love story, you think of your own past heartbreaks. When you watch a movie set in a high school, you can't help but remember your own experiences in high school. When you watch a sitcom about a family or group of friends, you think of the interactions of your own family and friends. Every time you watch a Christmas movie, you think of your own past Christmases.

It's no wonder that stories are how we connect with other people. It's how we empathize and it's how we evoke emotions.

I also know based on experience that this may sound daunting, so let me help you delve into whether *you are* a storyteller.

Are you a Storyteller?

I grew up thinking I didn't have any stories. Now, as you can see, I can't *stop* sharing my stories! It was a long journey for me to get to this point, however. No matter what setting I was in previously, I thought I didn't have anything worthy to say.

Whether that was in a classroom, not wanting to raise my hand. Whether that was in a group of people I had just met, thinking that I wasn't interesting enough to captivate a crowd. Whether that was at work, not wanting to interject with a different opinion… I never thought I had anything worthy to say. It took me until very recently - literally in the last year - to realize that I did.

Ok we're going to play another game!

You may have noticed that throughout this book, I have told many of my own stories. Because everything I have and am telling you to do on these pages are all things that I have either done or are doing.

And that includes storytelling. I've told you stories like the one about being posted on @foodgod, or the one about getting Puffington, or the one about my business mid-life crisis (as I like to call it), or the one about how The Choc Pot came to be.

Now I want you to ask yourself… Did you think these stories I've been telling were BIG moments in my life? Moments that are super different and super unique that they can *never* happen in your own lives?

Like you don't have a story about how you got your own pet, or started your business, or made a change or pivot in your business?

If you think that the moments I've spoken about are super BIG, so unique and different - that nothing I talk about could possibly happen in your own life, think "not me!".

If you think these were smaller, potentially everyday moments, ones that *could* happen in your life as well, think "me too!"

Hopefully this exercise worked 😄! Because what I want *all* of you to realize first and foremost is that even if you think *right now* that you aren't a storyteller - that you do not have any stories to tell - that by saying "me too!", it means that you do.

Because if *I* have stories I can tell, like how I got my cat of all things! Then I can guarantee that *you* have stories to tell.

So, are you a Storyteller? The answer is hands down, a resounding "YES!".

And yet… perhaps you don't believe me yet?

That's ok. Let's go through *how* you can become a storyteller, especially if you don't believe right now that you have any stories to tell.

Ask Yourself the Right Questions

I remember back when I was in corporate, for a period of time my desk was on the same floor as the Head of Banking & Financial Services, Greg Ward.

Being a morning person, I used to be one of the first people to get in really early. It's the best time to take stock and prepare myself for the day, not have to talk to anyone (come on now, you know I'm an introvert!), and make myself a quiet breakfast in the kitchen.

Every now and then, Greg would also be in the kitchen making his coffee.

I have the utmost respect for Greg - he is super smart, super focused and gets results. Yet, he wasn't a typical CEO. He was, in terms of knowing his numbers inside and out and rallying his team towards an outcome. But he wasn't in terms of the stereotypical smooth and polished leader we are used to seeing in the corporate world. He was actually quite an awkward conversationalist.

So just imagine the two of us introverts in the kitchen. One, a super senior and slightly awkward Executive. And the other, a young team member wanting to just get the heck out of there as quickly as possible before saying something really silly or stupid.

One morning there we were, doing our awkward shuffle around the kitchen and I thought to myself, "Well this is silly. We're the only people here and I should really say hello even if it's out of pure courtesy."

So, I asked him a general question - "How are you doing?" - so that I wouldn't sound silly or stupid.

His answer? "Good". And then he left.

The next day, the same thing happened. I asked him how he was, he said he was good and then he left.

So, this went on day after day until finally I decided to change it up. And I decided to ask him a more specific question. So instead of "How are you doing?" I asked him "What did you do over the weekend?"

It was definitely not a groundbreaking question, but it was a *different* question. And he started telling me about his weekend, the places he went to, the people he saw.

And so, I started asking him more detailed questions - about those places, about those people.

And we had a REAL conversation, and funnily enough, got to know each other a little. As much as you can in a 10-minute conversation in the kitchen! To the point that when I left corporate before moving to New York, he took me out for a farewell coffee.

I got to know some of his stories. About the time he held a party in his newly-renovated basement. About the fact that he's in a band (what?!). About his son struggling with school.

I now have so much respect for him, not because he knows how to run a business really effectively. But because he can do that *while being very human*.

And the only way I got to know this was because I started asking the right questions.

I know when I first started thinking I needed to tell my stories, I would try to look at my whole life and think "ok, what's something interesting I can talk about?"

How overwhelming! This was definitely NOT the right question to be asking.

So, then I started chunking it down. I started asking myself about a specific person, or place, or thing. I started asking myself about 'firsts' - the first time Ash and I met, the first time I got a pet, the first time I realized something important in my entrepreneurial journey.

I started thinking about times I felt strong emotions. The times I felt really upset, or overwhelmed, or down on myself, or like I was a failure… And also, the times I was euphoric, helpful and loved.

I started *seeing* and picking these moments in time - in my life - because I started asking myself the right questions.

So, there you go: *start asking yourself the right questions*. Start asking yourself questions about specific moments in time, and you will start to find your brain giving yourself the right answers. Answers that are linked to a story. Because our lives are just a sequence of stories.

By doing this, you are going to start to build a bank of stories.

Build Your Bank of Stories

You want to write down this bank of stories! Keep a record. It can be in a notebook, in a journal, on your phone.

I actually have a document on my phone with a running list of story ideas.

And the best format I've come across that works for me so that I can remember what the story is about is to actually write them down as episode titles. And specifically like the episode title of Friends.

For example:

1. The One Where the Monkey Gets Away
2. The One with Fake Monica
3. The One with the Breast Milk
4. The One with Five Steaks and an Eggplant
5. The One with the Baby on the Bus

That's seriously the easiest way I've found to do it, by writing it down as "the one with…"

- The One with Messagelytics
- The One with Finding Puffington
- The One with A Big Pot of Curry
- The One with the Decision to Move to NYC
- The One with My Secret Shame… Watching Keeping Up with The Kardashians

As you come across your stories, perhaps when you're on a run, or at the grocery store, or on the subway, write them down and build up your bank of stories.

Because then you'll find that you actually have a lot of inspiration to come back to! And all you have to do is find the right story to tell… a story that sells!

Writing a Story to Sell

How do you choose the right-fit stories?

I remember a couple of times when I was trying to do the networking thing, I was (unfortunately) *that* awkward person. The one who would join a small group of people and try to make myself visible. I would join in on the conversation and laugh along, all the while trying to frantically think of my own anecdote that I could share and contribute to the conversation.

And I tried! I would start telling a story and in my head it was making sense, but I'd also try to tell it quickly so that I didn't have too much attention on me and take up too much time. I'd start to ramble and lose the thread of why I even started going down this path, and then I'd just try to wrap it up really quickly.

And all this time, my heart is pounding, my mind is completely fuzzy and my face is burning. Yep, see what I mean about being that awkward person?

To the point that when I finished telling my anecdote, people would look at me in a politely curious way, thinking "What exactly was the point of that?"

Because the story just did not connect with them *or* the point it was trying to make.

Now while I'm still working on trying not to be *that* awkward person, you can see why choosing the right story is incredibly important. Because you want your stories to connect with your audience *and* to be relevant to the message you're trying to highlight.

Preferably, you don't want them leaving the conversation thinking "what was the point of that?"

So how do we do this? How do we choose the right story, and tell one that *sells*?

It starts with relevancy.

When you choose a story, the number one thing to keep in mind is whether it is relevant for your audience. Relevancy takes many forms, but a good yardstick to use to measure whether your story is going to be relevant to your audience is whether it *starts with the ordinary*.

Even if you have an extraordinary story to tell, can you make it relevant to your audience by starting with the ordinary? This is the only way you're going to have your story connect with them enough for them to want to hear the rest of it. This is why people love rags to riches stories, because almost everyone can relate (in some way) to the rags component - and so they are *able to consume* the story within their own frame - and then can't help also imagine what it would be like to grow to riches.

Being *able to consume* the story is how the connection is created. This is why telling ordinary, everyday stories is actually incredibly effective. Because even though *you* might think that it is 'everyday' (read: boring) for you, it is actually what makes you relatable to your audience and gets them to know, like and trust you.

So, when choosing a story, the first thing you want to consider is relevancy. The second thing you want to consider is the 'lesson' you want to share with your audience. I generally work backwards from the topic of what I'm sharing with my audience - which usually always stems from a winning Messagelytics result. For example, the topic could be about creating an effective hook, with one of the lessons or how-tos being about the pattern interrupt.

Topic: Creating an Effective Hook

Lesson: Pattern Interrupt

With this topic, I go back to my Episode Titles list of stories and see if I have one that unfolds into a message, moment of realization or analogy that I have about this topic or lesson.

I have a couple of options. I could, for example, tell 'The One with Messagelytics' and how this led us to coming up with some really effective hooks. However, if I go back to the first principle, how relevant would this story be to my audience? Perhaps for an audience that has been following me for a while and knows at least a little bit about Messagelytics and what it means, it could be super relevant. If I am talking to a relatively new audience, this would not be very relevant at all. They would have *no* idea about what I'm even talking about. I would probably not start with this particular story.

My second option is to tell 'The One with Finding Puffington' and how what he did was such an effective pattern interrupt that we knew he was the kitten for us. This is a very relevant, very ordinary moment that almost everyone can relate to and follow, either because they have a pet themselves, or know someone else who has a pet. So, when choosing a story to tell, think about 1) relevancy to your audience and whether it can immediately connect with them; and 2) the lesson you want to share and whether the story effectively unfolds into your lesson message.

Now you have your story, how do we structure it in a way that makes people want to take the next step with you?

Your Short Form Content Story Structure

I actually get asked this quite a bit which is honestly why I created the Capsho software. Because a lot of intelligent entrepreneurs already know that they need to be telling their stories in order to build connections. All of the marketing gurus tell us this.

But what they don't tell us is *how*. And specifically, *how* we tell our stories in short form content like Instagram or Facebook or TikTok captions. How exactly do we structure our stories effectively for short form content?

That's what I'll be sharing with you in this section.

Let's start with the types of characters in your story...

The first character is the hero.

The second character is the guide.

The third character is the pre-hero.

And this is how I want you to think about it: The hero of your story is going to be your dreamiest buyer, your ideal audience, the person you are trying to make a connection with. It is *not you*. It is *not your product or your offer*.

Because as I spoke about in the last section, we need to make your story relevant to your audience. Which means making *them* the hero of your story. When we can think about them being the hero, not us, then our minds already start to subconsciously make it relevant to them.

And I know what you might be thinking… "I'm telling a story about ME. How is someone else the hero of the story?" Amiright?

Ok, so let me explain how it all fits in…

You want to always be viewing your dreamiest buyer as the hero of your story because it has to be super relevant to them. But the other two character types - the guide and the pre-hero? They are *you*!

Your hero is at the start of their journey because they have a problem they need to solve, or they have an aspiration they'd like to reach. It could be that they need to lose weight, or grow their business. Or perhaps they want inspiring surroundings in their home, or to feel confident through the clothes they wear, or to show off their personality and individuality through their accessories. That's where they are right now, which makes them the hero. The story you're about to tell is actually about *them*.

I'd take a bet that whatever your story is about - it starts with someone who was exactly in your hero's predicament - with a problem they need solving or an aspiration they wanted to reach. And through their own journey, was able to reach that goal (or get closer to reaching that goal).

And I bet that more often than not, the someone in your hero's predicament, was most likely *you*. And that's why that makes you the *pre-hero*. The person who knows exactly what it feels, looks and sounds like to be in your hero's shoes. This is what makes you ordinary. Because you are *just like them*.

And because you have been able to journey through it, because you have been there and done that, it also makes you the *guide*. You are the Yoda to their Luke Skywalker, the Dumbledore to their Harry Potter, the Gandalf to their Frodo.

You can lay out the path for your hero and give them the map.

This is now what makes you extraordinary. This extraordinary-ness comes from the fact that you've been able to, or are in the process of solving for the problem you've identified, or the aspiration you're reaching for.

So, your story for short-form content starts with your pre-hero journey. Once you've established your ordinariness and relatability because you know exactly how it feels to be where they are right now, you then *flip* into your extraordinary-ness - into being the guide.

Let's start with how we tell the pre-hero's journey.

Telling the pre-hero's journey

You want to travel all the way back. Start at the very beginning of the story, when you first realized you had a problem, or when you knew something had to change.

What were you doing, thinking and feeling at that point, at the beginning of the story?

Write it down!

And then what prompted you to start to explore a change? What were you doing, thinking and feeling then?

A lot of times this is something external to us. For example, it could be someone we respect telling us we need to do something, or perhaps someone we love telling us something needs to change. It could also be something internal, where we wake up one day, feeling a certain way and knowing we need to do something about it.

So, what was it? What actually prompted you to start your journey and take the tangible steps towards your end result?

Now we want to think about what was in your way? What obstacles came up for you that made that change a little bit harder? What were you doing, thinking and feeling at that point?

Is it that you lost motivation at some point? Or perhaps the strategy you were implementing wasn't working?

And so, what did you do to overcome the obstacle? What happened? What was the result? What were you doing, thinking and feeling then?

If you lost motivation, how did you get it back to get to your result? If the original strategy you implemented wasn't working, how did you learn or come up with a new strategy that ended up working for you?

That is how you tell your pre-hero story. You can see that there's actually a little depth you need to go into. This is what creates the connection between you and your audience. They need to be able to see that you struggled through the same things that they are likely currently struggling through as well.

And when you can also talk about how you were *feeling*, this is when you bring your own emotions in. And when you can bring your emotions into your story, this is how you evoke emotions into your own audience. Storytelling like this is a neat way to cover off the first pillar of Honey Trap Marketing too!

Let's go through an example. I'm going to use one of my previous client's - Whitney's - story. Whitney has her own eCommerce brand selling candles.

"I was at work in the hospital, caring for my patients as a nurse. I love that I can help people, but the stress and the long hours were getting to me. I was missing being at home with my 1-year-old daughter, to the point where my arms actually ached from not being able to hold her [*beginning of the story - what was she thinking, feeling and doing at that time?*].

I had just left a patient's room when another nurse asked me a pretty simple question. Automatically, I found myself snapping at her and was appalled that I had made her cry. My face was burning with shame.

I knew then that something had to change. [*This moment is what prompted the change*].

I didn't know how to break out of this pattern, until my best friend gifted me a candle. When I lit it, I found myself almost immediately calming down, my breathing became deeper and slower, my eyes closed and peace settled over me.

I loved this feeling so much that I started looking for more candles, in particular scents I liked, but I just couldn't find them anywhere! [*This was the obstacle*].

And so, I started making them myself, researching the best blends for stillness, calm and peace. My hands were shaking with excitement the first time I nailed the perfect blend! [*Overcoming the obstacle*]."

Can you see how short and simple the story can be?

I'd like for you to give it a go now. Write out a pre-hero story about literally any topic that your audience cares about. This is how you do it.

So, you've told your pre-hero story. But you're not yet done. If we want to create content that sells, we now need to flip into the guide.

This is where the third pillar of creating Content Trust Accelerator comes in - providing practical value.

How Do We Provide Practical Value?

There was this time we were hiking up in New Hampshire and had caught up to the group who was in front of us on this downhill portion of the trek. We walked behind them for a couple of minutes and I happened to be eavesdropping on their conversation.

I thought they'd be talking about - I don't know - the beautiful weather, the scenery, getting away from the city.

But they weren't. They were talking about hair dryers.

Whether it was worth getting a Dyson, how much better could it be than another brand that can seemingly do the job just as well…

Can you believe it? There are a million and one other things they could be talking about… but hair dryers?

Although I really shouldn't judge because a friend of mine and I probably had a 30-40min chat about slow cookers… so definitely can't judge!

Now why of all things are we talking about hair dryers and slow cookers? Because of practical value.

People share practically valuable information to help others. People come to trust those that want to help them. Whether by saving a friend time or ensuring a colleague saves a couple of dollars the next time she goes to the supermarket, useful information helps.

That's why in our content, we go from telling the pre-hero journey and flip into being the guide. So how do we do that?

We need to now share what we actually learnt from the journey we went through, the pre-hero story we shared.

What was your realization? Your change in perspective? What can you tangibly share with your own audience so that they can make a similar mindset or implementation shift from reading your tips?

In this part, I generally share three tips. The human brain can rarely consume any more than that, so we want to keep it to three tips, each with an example.

I would also recommend (as long as it makes sense), to use the last tip to "sell" something. It might be a product, or it may even be a free lead magnet. If you have effectively created a connection with your dreamiest buyer and they want to continue the relationship with you, this is when you want to nudge them to do so.

Content Trust Accelerators is just one half of an effective and enticing feed.

Like any good healthy personal relationship, you need the other side. For example, for a strong and healthy bond with your partner, you want to create **love** through intimacy, shared vulnerabilities and familiarity (i.e., Content Trust Accelerator) *and* **desire** through space, anticipation and mystery (i.e., Content Honey Traps).

We've just covered how to produce that trust and love through Content Trust Accelerators. Let's now get into how to create the desire - Content Honey Traps.

Creating Your Content Honey Traps

Content Honey Traps are a system of *reconceptualized* (not repurposed) content designed to compel your dreamiest clients to follow you through your front-end funnel - from your social media to a piece of long-form content (e.g., podcast or blog) to your conversion event - so that you have a consistent stream of buyers waiting to throw their credit cards at you!

In this system, you are capturing people's attention and setting "honey traps" throughout to create *so much* curiosity in your audience that compels them to stay with you.

Why do we want to set honey traps?

Contrary to popular belief, the chances of someone seeing a piece of content you put out and buying something straight away is almost zero to none (unless we're talking about quite an inexpensive product) . So instead, we want to be leading your buyers down a path that will lead to monetization. We want to be focused on the long-game, with any immediate conversions being a bonus.

We are going to lead your dreamiest buyers down a path and into "honey traps" so that after 7 hours with you, it's a no-brainer for them to buy your offer. Because through these 7 hours, you've built 1) know; 2) like; and 3) trust. And how we're going to do this is through a mix of short-form, long-form and interactive content.

Creating an array of short-form content is designed to get you *known*. If you can be visible on a consistent basis to your dreamiest buyers, then you are building recognizability. The type where they can't help but say "I feel like I know you already!", even when they've never met you before.

Creating long-form content is designed to get you *liked*. By sharing more with your audience so that they spend more time with you, you almost become part of their family. I once had a client tell me her young daughter had started practicing her Australian accent because of how much of my long-form content (videos and podcasts) were getting played. It was like I was a part of the family!

Your short-form content should be leading your audience into your long-form content (and vice versa). These are your "honey traps", with both leading to your interactive content. Interactive content is content designed to encourage interaction between yourself, your audience and each other. This might be via email or through another closed community platform.

A mix of this content will get you your 7 hours relatively quickly. And this will, in turn, earn you even more *trust*.

For illustration purposes, I'm going to run through a very round-numbered example. Let's say you create a 1-minute video every day that you share on social media. You have 1,000 followers and your content is surfaced to say 10% of them, so 100 people. That is potentially 100 people watching 5 minutes of your content every week. From your short-form content, you want to be leading your audience to your long-form content. Let's say your long-form content is 30 minutes. This means each episode will make a 7% dent in the 7 hours required for lifelong trust. Releasing an episode each week will mean you could have raving fans in ~12 weeks. This can be further shortened if they join your community and consume your emails or engage with you and each other in another community-based platform. Let's say that's 45 minutes a week in total. 45 minutes a week and you'll have 100 very engaged, very loyal followers in around 9 weeks.

With an ever-growing backlog of content, your new audience has even more content to consume and engage with. After they come to know, like and trust you they will become a buyer of yours.

This is how *Content Honey Traps* work.

So, let's see how we create it.

We start with creating long-form content using the three pillars of Content Trust Accelerators - evoking emotions, storytelling and practical value. If you can practice these, you have the backbone to create content that connects. I find it is generally easier to start with long-form content when doing this - either a podcast, a YouTube video or a blog.

We then look at that piece of long-form content and work out what the best piece of it is. What is the part that provides the most value, the biggest "aha", the best tip, for your audience? Now we do *not* want to share that. We just want to base our "honey trap" on that part because our aim is to create so much curiosity about this piece in our social media that it pushes people to have to consume your long-form content (remember we're clocking up our 7 hours!)

Knowing what it is you *don't* want to share; how can you create so much curiosity about it in your short-form content that people will be CLAMORING to want to listen or read about it? This is how we reconceptualize, not repurpose!

The way we think about doing this is through eight specific mental models. Your Content Honey Traps can be based on either the 'story' component of your long-form content, or the 'value/tips' component. There are four mental models for each. Let me outline those to you:

Story-based Content Honey Traps

Content Honey Trap name	Definition
The Paradox	Intrigue your audience by contrasting the big result you achieved with a surprising or unbelievable fact
The Cliffhanger	Tempt your audience by sharing the most dramatic moment of your story, leaving them hanging about what happens next!
The Big Reveal	Lure your audience in by hinting at the unexpected twist in your story
The Sharer	Whet your audience's appetite for the full details of your story by giving away the ending

Value-based Content Honey Traps

Content Honey Trap name	Definition
The Rebel	Draw your audience in by alluding to myths you're busting
The Jawdropper	Entice your audience by teasing a secret you're delving into
The Marvel	Entice your audience by teasing a framework (with a cool name) that you're delving into
The Boxer	Compel your audience by agitating the pain points they are feeling and hinting at the solution you are sharing

Using these mental models will enable you to create intense curiosity in your "honey traps". "Honey traps" to move your audience to your next piece of content… so that they spend at least 7 hours with you! Think about how you can create this curiosity in interesting ways with your content - with your captions, your graphics, your Reels, videos, etc. Just remember: Never give the answer away!

Accelerating Your Content Honey Traps (In Less Than 5 Mins a Week)

I've just shared with you my entire blueprint on how to think through and create your short form Content Trust Accelerators and Content Honey Traps from scratch - anchored in the three fundamental pillars of evoking emotions, storytelling and providing practical value.

But are you perhaps thinking that this all still sounds a little too hard? I know I get it!

Creating content is important. Creating content is the primary way for you to increase your credibility and authority. When people go to Google you or find you on social media, they're going to look at your content. They're going to want to see what you do, what your values are and importantly, what value you can provide them.

Which is why I went through the three pillars of creating your Content Trust Accelerators - evoking emotions, storytelling and practical value. If you can practice these, then it doesn't matter what happens to each platform, you have the backbone to creating content that connects and sells.

So yes, creating content is important.

But is it worth spending hours and hours to create content hoping that you will be able to create trust? No.

Which is why we created our AI-driven software, Capsho. I wanted a way to very quickly create everything business owners need to distribute and promote their long-form content and grow their list.

For example, if your long-form content is your podcast episode, Capsho will automatically generate episode title, player descriptions, show notes, episode social media captions and promotional emails with Content Honey Traps.

If you want to give it a test drive, try it at www.capsho.com.

How to Create Posts That Will Stop the Scroll

I've laid out the complete strategy to create captions for your Content Trust Accelerators and Content Honey Traps, however this chapter would not be complete without going into creating the visuals or creatives for your posts.

You want creatives that will "stop the scroll" - gain the attention of your audience either on their feed as they're scrolling down, or on the explore page for potentially new eyeballs.

There is a *lot* of experimentation when creating graphics. But like with everything I go through, there is a really effective way of not having to start from absolute zero when thinking about what creatives to produce.

It's through using a simple methodology called Content Hacking.

The idea behind Content Hacking is something Tony Robbins and Russell Brunson have drilled into me. As Tony Robbins says, "Success leaves clues". So, we want to see what others are doing to create success with their content, and then we want to follow or model it.

And please note that we're very deliberately saying "modeling" and not "copying".

Content Hacking is simply finding posts from accounts your dreamiest buyers are following and using these as inspiration. The words and the images, however, will be completely our own.

We are just going to see what has worked for others, why that may have been and how we can recreate our own version.

The way I determine appropriate content to hack is:

1. Find an account your dreamiest buyers are following. This is important because remember that what might work for one type of person may not work for another. You want to try to hack

content that you have a pretty good idea that is already resonating with your audience.

2. On that account, you want to find a particular post that has combined engagement (likes and comments) that is around double, or more than double the other posts around it.

3. Ask yourself what you think it was about that creative that stopped the scroll in order to gain that much more engagement.

4. Create your own version of it. And when you're doing this, you can 100% reconceptualize some of Capsho's outputs for your visuals. For example, you can shoot a short video, Reel or TikTok based on the story you input into Capsho. You can use some of the copy outputs from Capsho as the text overlays on your creatives (e.g., on Reels or for your quote posts).

Here is an example of when we content hacked @garyvee on Instagram. We found a post that did particularly well - a vimage (an animated image) with a motivational quote on it. We created our own version with a totally different vimage and quote. The quote was part of a story that I had put into Capsho, so it also integrated well into the post's caption that I lifted out of Capsho.

How did this post perform? It similarly performed above average (at least double the other posts around it) in terms of engagement on my account as well!

Here is @garyvee's post we content hacked:

This is the post we created:

Content Hacking can work for any platform. I showed examples on Instagram; however, we use this exact same strategy for TikTok, Facebook, YouTube. Any platform you are creating content for, rest assured you can use this strategy, which means that you will already have a head start in creating your Content Honey Traps.

If you listen to any of the TikTok gurus, they tell you to follow the trends. If there's a trending piece of audio, you want to use that. What they are doing with this strategy is Content Hacking! The only difference is, I want you to be more strategic and care about *who* is actually engaging with that content. Creating something viral for the sake of that "number of views" vanity metric is not worth your time. You're a Sloth Boss, so I know you're smarter than that. Content Hack based on your dreamiest buyers!

Now that we have you building credibility and authority and creating strong connections with your dreamiest buyers through your Content Trust Accelerators and Content Honey Traps, let's get you more eyeballs. Let's get visibility and leads!

This comes down to the third variable of The Honey Trap Formula: Traffic.

5.
BUILDING YOUR TRIBE WITH THE TRAFFIC PYRAMID

My head was in my hands as I looked at our bank account. I had to make the hard call; something, anything to stop the bleeding from continuing to happen. I should have known better. But there I was with our credit card bill in hand. Line after line read: "FACEBOOK…" We had racked up over $1200 in ad spend, without making any money. How was that possible?

I felt stupid, silly, like a complete failure. How is it that we were making tens of thousands of dollars from ads for our clients, but we couldn't get it right for our own business?

Let me rewind a little and explain.

I had just moved to New York. My co-founder, Bona, and I had just decided to close up shop on the fashion-tech business we had been working on while we were still in Sydney. While we were trying to decide our next move, I bumped into an acquaintance, someone I met through a mutual friend from when I was still in corporate. We got to chatting. He told me he was looking to expand his brick & mortar retail chocolate store online. He knew my background growing The Choc Pot, and invited me to help him with his online presence through digital marketing.

Bona and I worked on the account and were blown away with our results. Soon after, I started reaching out to some other boutiques and online businesses and we had a few clients on board who we were doing agency work for. And we were making them a ton of money! After a few months, we decided, "Why not start our own e-commerce business and we could make *even more* money?!"

We knew that with the success we'd already helped these other brands achieve, there was absolutely no way we could fail! Doing the same for ourselves as we were doing for our clients was going to be easy, we thought.

We dug out Bona's home-made skincare formulations, did some research to stabilize them, got ourselves some fancy bottles and packaging, and set up a website. Then we created some (in my opinion) pretty awesome ads!

I was struggling to contain my excitement because I couldn't wait to see the money rolling in! These ads were going to be the silver bullet to growth, sales and success! I couldn't wait! We turned them on and waited.

Ok… nothing yet… that's fine, we just need to give it a few days so that the algorithm can learn… Still nothing. Ok? We tweaked our creative (text and images) so we could grab people's attention. We got some new followers on our page, but no sales!? We changed our copy, had some click through to our website, *but still, no sales*. What was going on!? We looked at everything. We were doing this successfully for all these other brands. Why wasn't it working for ours? We were tweaking our ads until we no longer had any more money to test with. After wasting all this money on ads and not getting many sales, we turned them off and tried to work out what was going on.

And then it hit me: when we compared the performance of our business with the brands we were working with. The one obvious thing that stood out was that those brands already had an audience. *They already had customers*. They had put some time and effort into getting a pool of buyers without the ads. And only now were they reinvesting into ads with a proven audience. And we hadn't done that yet. That was the step we had completely missed. By that point, we had no more money to spend on ads and I had to figure out another way. In my desperation, I started finding individuals on social media I thought would be absolutely ideal buyers of ours. I reached out to them individually through my social media accounts, having conversations with them to find out what was working for them and what wasn't. Before I knew it, we had people buying! I was making sales, and I wasn't even spending any money on ads! I knew then that I had cracked a code, yet didn't quite know how to articulate it. Then, something magical happened… in the shower.

For whatever strange reason, I get my best ideas in the shower. Too much information? Sorry, but it's true! Showers are actually a creative marketing strategy at *Capsho* :).

One morning, I was holding a marketing strategy session (aka taking a shower) and I was thinking about the day ahead. That day, I was hosting the *3-day Cold to Converted Challenge* for The Growth Boss, and something was bothering me, but I couldn't pinpoint what it was. You know that feeling, where you've been working on something for a long time and it's good enough. Yet, your intuition tells you that you're only a little tweak away from turning that into something *great*!? It was one of those moments.

When I asked the question about what our group was currently doing to get traffic to their websites, everyone across the map said "I'm on Instagram and Facebook." Then, as I prodded some more, a few others said "Oh yeah, I also work with some Influencers on Instagram." Then an even smaller subset said, "I've also tried Facebook ads but they just don't work." Then I had a massive *aha moment*.

These conversations were highlighting a traffic *pyramid;* a progression of tiers, or *phases*. These are specific marketing activities *all business owners* do in order to master their traffic and build their tribe. These tiers are sequential. Meaning: in most cases, you'll move up the pyramid in step-by-step order. Yet, it is also cyclical. As in: when you're mastering a different channel (like going from Facebook to Instagram) you can move between each tier, depending on what you want for your situation. This is what we want to be doing as we build out our traffic machine. If you follow the strategy I'm about to lay out, you can build your own audience of ideal buyers without spending any money on ads first. That way, you can cost-effectively scale when you are ready to invest in ads.

I'm going to show you a step-by-step process for gaining a tremendous amount of market research that you can apply to your advertising. The best part is: you'll be making money as you learn, as opposed to spending money to learn. You'll be testing and iterating your brand personality and the types of content that resonate. You'll be leveraging other people's audiences and tracking which influencers drive the most qualified traffic to your website, sales page or social media accounts. You'll know how to analyze your results. Here it is…

[Pyramid diagram with tiers from top to bottom: PAID, LEVERAGE AUDIENCES, ACTIVE ORGANIC, PASSIVE ORGANIC]

Passive Organic Marketing. This is the first tier and something I have already covered in quite some detail in the previous chapter. If you're "just on" any one of the major platforms, you're doing Passive Organic Marketing. Also, it's not *passive* in the sense that you're not doing anything. You may be consistently posting your *Content Trust Accelerators* and *Content Honey Trap* material on Instagram for instance, or creating podcast content, which is hardly sitting back and doing nothing. That's real work. What I mean by the word *passive* is that you're waiting for your customer to stumble upon you, *hoping* they'll find your content and you.

One of the best parts of Passive Organic Marketing that I've already mentioned is that you're developing your voice and building your credibility for people to snoop through when they arrive on your profile or page.

Active Organic Marketing. You have created your content, and now it's time to have it working for you. This is all about knowing how to use each channel to its fullest capability. You're intentionally creating reach, engagement and visibility for your content and your business. You're starting to build your audience at an individual level and cultivating relationships with them. All so you can build a tribe of qualified leads. This strategy in itself could be a profit center in your business and is actually the main way we still generate leads (more on this later). Meaning, you can set up a daily habit (or standard operating system if you have a team), and use this strategy to generate leads completely organically.

Leveraging other people's audiences. This is where you are collaborating with someone else who has a large audience that you're tapping into, and drawing that audience back into your world. One part of it is what we might commonly refer to as *Influencer Marketing*, however as I'll expand upon, there are a host of other types of people (like anyone in your Dream100), audiences, and ways you can be leveraging!

The bottom line is that here, you are entering into the influencer's world. Sometimes that's doing a co-hosted live, being interviewed on a podcast, having the Influencer/Dream100 send out an email, a shout-out, or sharing your videos/content in some capacity. It doesn't matter what platform they're on, as long as they are sending that traffic back to you and your lead magnet.

One of the things you should understand before getting into influencer marketing is this: it is a volume game. A single reference is likely not going to transform your business overnight. With a large enough group of Influencers/Dream 100, however, their powers combined create an almost compound interest effect on your exposure. Your potential buyers start thinking, "Why is this person showing up everywhere?" And it's because you've gotten crystal clear on the types of Influencers/Dream 100 you want associated with your brand, that have the right audience for you, and you have created these connections with the Influencers and your Dream 100.

Paid Ads. You've done the hard work. You've organically built your audience of ideal buyers and you can now reinvest into paid advertising to really scale. Having said that, paid ads are a whole new ball game that need a strategy of their own as well as some time and money for experimentation. The key is to be strategic with this testing, use the data to learn more about your audience and optimize your ads accordingly.

Next, we're going to break down each tier of the Traffic Pyramid. As we've already covered Tier #1 - Passive Organic Marketing - in the last chapter, we're going to be starting with Tier #2 - Active Organic Marketing. I encourage you to go through and implement these in the order they are presented. Think of this like an investment portfolio that attracts compound interest.

But first… Where Do I Build My Tribe?

My friend, Yen, and I were both in our second year of university working on an entrepreneurship competition (talk about being a nerd, right?). It was the middle of summer, and we were at Yen's house with four other people. The plan was that all six of us would hop in the pool, because we had to stay cool to be productive, naturally. Then, we would get on with the rest of the assignment.

As we were bobbing in the water, we somehow got to talking about this new thing called "Facebook." Yen had just been recently invited. It really was back in the OG days when you had to be in university/college and actually be invited to be able to set up an account. Everyone was clamoring for an invite! No one really knew what it was, but the exclusivity had massive appeal.

After signing up, it was a bit of fun finding other people on there from high school, "friend requesting" them, posting all the photos and doing the tagging thing… and then I lost interest.

It was only a few short years, and many iterations of Facebook later, when I had started my first business that I recalled the updated functionality of being able to start a business page.

I knew the basics of how the platform worked and I'd actually accumulated quite a few friends on there, so I started the business page and invited all of my friends to like it.

Unbeknownst to me, that would be my first foray into some form of viral marketing. Because from there, my friends invited their friends to like it, and it grew organically from there. We didn't even have great content. It was all completely passive organic marketing but we had ridden the growth wave of Facebook. Mind blown!

A few months later, Anne, one of our casual staff members, who was still in high school asked me if we were on Instagram. I had NO IDEA what she was talking about. It was one of those few times that I felt incredibly old as a young person. So, she grabbed my phone, and set The Choc Pot up with a profile. The photos were ugggly! But we were on there and her instructions were, "Just keep posting photos." So, we did. To this day, I still credit Instagram as one of the main reasons we were able to grow quickly. We had people come to our little store from the other side of Sydney mentioning that they found out about us through Instagram. It was insane! All we were doing was posting photos (passive organic marketing) but we had ridden the growth wave of Instagram.

For some reason I've been fortunate enough to ride the growth wave of two of the biggest social media platforms with my first business. Completely passively and organically. I thought it would be the same with my second, and third, and fourth business. But let me tell you: it hasn't.

I have struggled since then to be able to post something and get the types of reach, likes, follows, and engagement I had easily with my first business. We have to realize: as platforms grow and evolve and search for monetization, our ability to reach a large audience organically will change and shrink as per their algorithms. Now, we have to be intentional with how we utilize these platforms, and be open to shifting with the platform as they do. More importantly, we have to be intentional with the outcome that we are looking to get from these platforms.

As time has gone on, I've borne witness to many friends, acquaintances and other business owners having pages shut down, ads accounts shut down, being told what they can and can't post. What this has been highlighting is the risk in putting all our eggs into the social media basket. For example, if Instagram is your main way of getting traffic and your account gets shut down... where is that going to leave you and your business? How will you be able to continue generating leads in order to make sales?

Let's be intentional with what outcome we are looking to get from these platforms. And that outcome? It is going to be to build your email list. Because your email list will always be something that you own.

Your email list is going to be the tribe we are building.

Once they're on your email database, you can then nurture them into the sale. I cover this in more detail in my book for eCommerce business owners - *The Conversion Formula*.

Building your email list is going to be one of your most valuable assets in business. Building an email list means you will be future-proofing your business, because you won't be at the mercy of the platform's ever-changing algorithms and rules. You won't be at the mercy of an account shut-down or blocked ads.

Whichever platform/s you decide to be on, you need to think strategically about how you are going to guide and magnetize your dreamiest buyers onto your email list. The first step is to know *how* to do this - that is what The Traffic Pyramid will take you through. The last chapter covered the bottom tier, Passive Organic Marketing, and how to create your Content Trust Accelerators and Content Honey Traps. With that in mind, we are now going to get into the second tier of The Traffic Pyramid, Active Organic Marketing.

Tier 2: Active Organic Marketing

There were exactly 2 minutes left on the clock and I watched in horror as the thing we had to stop at all costs was happening.

The woman in the green shorts (we didn't know her name), had broken free of the line and was sprinting down the field.

This was it… was our season over?

Let me back up a little and explain.

Our mixed Oztag team had actually made the Grand Final. For the uninitiated, Oztag is an Australian sport similar to Flag Football - with the tags - but playing Rugby League rules instead. On a mixed team, there are four women and four men that play on the field for each team.

It was our first season playing in Division 1, the top division. We had just been bumped up from Division 2 and had lost game after game. But somehow, we started winning games (by very close margins), clawed our way into the Finals and, surprisingly, made it to the Grand Final game!

I'm not sure any of us knew how we did it, but here we were playing in the Grand Final.

And even better, we were actually up by 1! Currently winning by just 1 slim point. With 2 minutes to go.

Our friends on the sidelines were going crazy with excitement, jumping up and down and yelling all sorts of encouragement and strategies that I couldn't hear from across the field.

The other team's fans were likewise on their feet, on tenterhooks.

And that was when she made the break. Our whole game plan had been to shut her down. We knew she was the most dangerous player on the team. Great with the ball, fast and it helps that when a woman scores, they get awarded 2 points instead of just 1 (call that positive discrimination?)

That had been our focus all game and it was working. We were up by 1 with 2 minutes left.

Until she made that break. And I could feel myself physically deflating. All the blood, sweat and tears we had put into the other 38 minutes of the game going up in flames.

When suddenly - and I couldn't believe my eyes - but Chris on our team had just run her down and tagged her! He had saved the game for us!

The crowd on the sideline went crazy. I sprinted back into the line where she had been tagged.

They moved the ball; we defended the next play and the referee finally blew the Full-Time whistle.

Our team roared with success and our friends ran over to hug us. We had won the game! We had actually won the game!! I still couldn't believe it. I carried that high with me for weeks afterwards.

And even now, thinking about it makes me smile. And I'm not even sure if it's just because of the win that I smile about. Perhaps it's more about how we came together and hustled as a team to make it happen.

We were not meant to have made the Grand Final. We were the underdogs, just like how we feel like we're the underdogs now in the social media world. But against all odds we had done it. And even better, we knew going into the Grand Final game what we needed to do.

We were up by 1 and as a team, we had one focus, and one focus only. Shut the woman with the green shorts down. We knew if we could do that, we were in with a fighting chance.

And we did!

So, in that same vein, how do you give your content a fighting chance? Even as the underdog? How do you create that kind of laser focus to enable your content to help you and your business get the reach and visibility you deserve? So that you can win and keep winning?

How do you turn your traditionally "passive" marketing *active*?

Let me first explain why the bottom of the Traffic Pyramid is called Passive Organic Marketing.

In the last chapter, I spoke about the importance of you creating your content. As an entrepreneur, you cannot get away from it. It is how you build credibility and authority; it is how you become known, liked and trusted, and it is how your dreamiest buyers may come to first find out about you.

However, creating and posting content in and on its own is "passive" because you've probably released it into the world with no real strategy about how you're going to have people see it. How you're going to make it truly visible.

That would be like us entering that Grand Final game without a strategy on how we might even win the darn thing. Letting ourselves passively play the game and just hoping for a good outcome.

And I know I'm not being fair because I get it… it is a LOT of work creating all that content. But I do not want you to be creating content for content's sake.

So, what I want to talk about is how we turn this passive activity - of creating content and posting on social media - into an active activity. What do we need to do to ensure that you work your way to the win? To get the reach and visibility that you and your content deserves?

It comes down to the data.

Just like how as a team in the game we had focus. So, will you.

We knew - with 2 minutes left of the game, being 1 point down - we knew EXACTLY what we had to do. That was our data. The time left and the scoreboard was our data.

And with that data we had a strategy and a sole focus. Shut the woman with the green shorts down. And as a team, we were almost maniacal in fulfilling that strategy.

We won the game.

So that is how I want you to think about turning your passive content active. We are no longer going to just put content out there, hoping that someone happens to stumble across it somewhere, somehow.

No. We are going to get intelligent about the data and what we do with that data so that we give ourselves that fighting chance every single time of getting our content (and therefore our businesses) in front of our dreamiest buyers.

It comes down to these three metrics: Reach, Engagement, Qualified Followers.

Let me now break each down for you.

Reach

Let's start with Reach.

I have a love/hate relationship with Reach because I'm a little bit of a control freak and I don't like the fact that there is something that is a little out of my control.

But I also know how important this is as a metric because otherwise how else can we have that fighting chance of getting our content in front of your new dreamiest buyers?

So, what I'm going to do is talk about how we track reach and what we do about it, but I preface this by saying that a lot of it is also unfortunately outside of our control.

Reach is the number of accounts (or people) that have seen your content. At the time of writing this book, if we're talking Instagram and YouTube, the main data point we're looking at is "Impressions". On TikTok it is "Reached Audience".

So, for the platforms that you are on, what are the metrics telling you about how much reach your content is getting? You want to start with a baseline. *Your* baseline. And you just want to ensure that you're tracking which way your content is trending from there in terms of reach.

Now, how do you actually influence the reach of your content? This is definitely going to depend on the platform.

For example, at the time of writing this book, we know that hashtags do play a part with your reach on Instagram. We know this because you can see that data point on each post as part of the insights they provide. You'll see the number of accounts reached, the % of those that aren't currently following you and the number of impressions from your hashtags.

So, if you can, experiment with the hashtags you're using and my recommendation is to stick to ones that only have around 10,000 - 200,000 posts using them. This is because as your account is growing, your post will be drowned out if you use hashtags that are any larger than this.

If you're looking to increase reach on YouTube, this is going to come down to the SEO being optimized in your title and the eye-catchiness of your thumbnail. If you're looking to increase reach on TikTok, the main thing we're experimenting with right now is increasing the % number of people who watch the full video. This tells the algorithm that your content is valuable to more people, which means the platform will want to share it with more people.

As I mentioned, I do have a love/hate relationship with Reach, so should you pull your hair out trying to increase this metric? My personal opinion is that while it's definitely important to know the driving factors behind Reach, I wouldn't recommend you put most of your eggs in this basket. Instead, I would prefer you focus on the second metric - Engagement.

Engagement

Engagement is a great way to measure the *quality of your content*.

Because it is the quality of your content that is going to drive the quality of your followers. And as you'll learn when I talk about Active Organic Marketing, the quality of your followers will drive the quality of your leads.

Quality of Content → Quality of Followers → Quality of Leads

So how do you know whether the content you are producing is quality? Through engagement. Driving engagement is useful for a couple of reasons - the first is to help *you* to know whether your content is actually valuable to your followers.

You can then use this to make informed decisions about what type of content around what topics you should be producing going forward.

The second is to help the *algorithm* know who they should put your content in front of.

You'll notice that your posts will not be put in front of *all* of your followers, right? As the platform grows with more and more people and businesses jumping on, it just physically cannot handle being able to put your content in front of *all* of your followers, especially when most people are following hundreds, if not thousands of other accounts.

But it *will* put your content in front of people who tell the platform that they like your content.

This is why tracking and driving engagement is particularly important.

The data you want to be looking at here for Instagram are likes, comments, saves and shares. For TikTok it is likes, comments and shares. For YouTube, I would focus on the end screen click-through-rate.

So, you want to be looking at the total engagement rate on the % of followers you have.

If you see a particular piece of content do extremely well, what can you take from that and do more of? If you see a post that didn't do so well, why? What was it about the creative or the copy that did not help that post?

Going back to the previous chapter on creating your Content Honey Traps will give you the starting point.

I want you to focus more on increasing your engagement with your existing followers than on increasing your reach because the quality of your content is going to drive the number of qualified followers you get on your account.

The number of qualified followers is important because this is what is going to drive your number of qualified leads. And THIS is ultimately what we want out of our social media activity. Leads for you to convert into cold hard cash.

The Number of Qualified Followers

Let's now cover the number of qualified followers as a metric and how we increase this.

Now, note that I did not say to increase the number of your followers *period*. They MUST be *qualified followers* - people who are in YOUR target market and are your dreamiest buyers. Because having followers for followers sake will not move the dial for you and your business.

So here, the metric you want to be looking at is the number of qualified followers you have as a % of your total no. of followers. To do this, we have a spreadsheet where we keep track of all these potential "leads" we have - we haven't converted them into a genuine lead yet (as in an email on our database), but we have a plan to!

How do we increase the number of qualified followers we have on our account?

Well, when any of us make a decision to follow a brand-new account, what factors do we consider?

I don't know about you, but the first place I look is that person's bio. Are they doing something and will they be talking about things that I'm going to care about? (Let me throw in a tip here: Messagelytics can help you with this!)

The second thing I'll look at is the quality of the content. Are they actually producing content that will connect with me and provide me with value? That is why I go back to Engagement as one of the top metrics to stay on top of, because as you can see, the quality of your content will drive the number of qualified followers.

And once you have these followers, our job is to convert these followers into leads. And from there, to convert these leads into buyers.

So how do we even get these followers to know about us in the first place? One is through Reach, which I've already spoken about. And as you know by now, I'm not always a fan of dwelling on this particular metric because of the lack of control we have here. It's kind of like commissioning a billboard ad on a highway. The ad will "reach" x number of people driving up and down that highway through their eyes flicking over it (i.e., "impression"). How many of these eyeballs are going to be your dreamiest buyers? Who in the world knows?! That's how much control we have over a metric like Reach.

So, the other means that I prefer to use to increase the number of my qualified followers is through Targeted Conversations. This is where we take that control back into our own hands and *deliberately* get ourselves in front of the right people. Doing this means you no longer have to rely on *hope* as your marketing strategy.

Once I made these changes, I started seeing significant returns from social media, making me consistently over 5-figures a month. In fact, some of my BEST clients came in this way because they were all completely qualified. I'm going into more detail on how to do this in the section on Targeted Conversations.

For now, let's focus on how we optimize the engagement metric.

Optimizing Your Engagement

When it comes to Honey Trap Marketing, a crucial step is to always be optimizing based on data, which will help you make the intelligent decisions to keep moving forward.

The most straightforward way to optimize the engagement metrics on your content is to think about just three things:

1. Hook
2. Story
3. Call-to-action

Let's start with your hook. For your content, your hook is made up of two things: *your creative* and *the first line of your caption*.

To recap, when I say "your creative", I'm referring to the image, graphic, reel, video that you are using as the visual component of your post. The image has to be compelling enough to your audience to "stop the scroll". It has to hook them in! I've already provided you with a foolproof strategy to give yourself a head start here - Content Hacking. If you're finding that your impressions are dropping, you may want to have another look at how you can increase the scroll-stopping power of your creative.

Once you have compelled your audience enough to stop-the-scroll, their eyes will immediately go to the first line of your caption - to the part that is visible, before they have to hit "more" to expand the rest of the caption. They will ONLY hit "more" if that visible first line is compelling enough for them to do so, because again, you've hooked them in. The best way to hook someone is to *intrigue them*, to stir up so much curiosity, leave them on a cliffhanger that they NEED to know what happens next.

If the hook of your caption's first line does not compel your audience to click "more", you will find that engagement will be a lot lower. Your hook (or variations of your hook) can be derived from the Messagelytics process I have already covered.

Let's now turn our attention to the second optimization component - story.

Again, I have laid out the strategy for you to think about, find and write your story in previous lessons of this challenge. The story component of your caption is going to be what connects with your audience enough for them to care about what you have to say.

When you can create this connection through evoking emotions and providing practical value, your audience will be compelled into action.

Which leads me to the last part of optimizing engagement - the call-to-action.

You need to tell your audience what you want them to do. A mistake I see people make is that they *assume* their audience knows what they want them to do. This is incorrect. You want to make it so stupidly simple for your audience to take the next action that their brain and fingers automatically do it.

So, tell them. That's the first way to make it stupidly simple.

The second way is to make the call-to-action as bite-sized as possible. We have been experimenting with decreasing the cognitive load with our asks in order to increase engagement.

For example, we started with bigger asks like: "tell me about a time you also felt this way." Too big and too general.

So, then we started paring it back to the point where we were just telling people to: "drop a 🔥 if you agree."

Play around with your call-to-action and see how you can make yours stupidly simple for your audience. Assess whether you're then able to increase engagement.

As a complement to Honey Trap Marketing, we designed software called Capsho for the exact purpose of making the content creation and optimization process a lot simpler and easier.

Of course, you don't have to use Capsho. Based on what I've already outlined in this book, you are already armed with all the tools and knowledge you need to manually create engaging and optimized content on your own.

Keep in mind that optimization is (unfortunately) a never-ending process, it is never set-and-forget. You might find something works really well for you one week, and then suddenly it doesn't work anymore.

This is completely (even if infuriatingly) normal.

You can imagine why things never stay the same. We're talking about the combination of human behavior, platform changes and algorithms. Put these into a melting pot and it's no surprise that you're going to have to constantly stay on top of optimizing your metrics, especially engagement.

Do this, and you'll be able to bask in that glow of progress, momentum and results!

Explore vs. Search-Based Platforms

We have so far covered how to turn your traditionally passive content into active content on social media. Social media platforms like Instagram, Facebook and TikTok are commonly known as *demand creation* or *explore-based* platforms.

They are first and foremost "discovery" platforms, meaning they are about providing entertainment, news, or a place where people might stumble upon something fascinating. We have already covered what you need to do to create scroll-stopping and engaging content for these platforms.

Search-based or platforms that *meet demand* are platforms people visit with an intention. They type something in to get some type of result. Examples of search-based platforms are Google, YouTube, Pinterest and any Podcasting apps (e.g., Apple iTunes, Spotify, Stitcher, etc.).

These platforms are result-oriented, which is why demand-meeting platforms are based on the keyword or search engine optimization (SEO) strategy. I am not going to go into the ins and outs of search engine optimization in this book, although you can grab a list of recommended tools for keyword research at:

www.deirdretshien.com/resources.

The key is to know the differences in approach you need to have based on the platforms you are using. If you are just starting out, I would recommend that you start with just one explore-based and one search-based platform. By focusing on just one in each to begin with, you will be able to very quickly repurpose content across platforms.

For example, by starting on Instagram, you will be creating image, graphic and video-based content. To get started on the other explore-based platforms like Facebook and TikTok, you could simply reuse this content until you've implemented the systems that will help you create the time you need to produce original content for each platform (if you should choose to do so).

For search-based platforms, as an example, you could start by podcasting. You could then create show notes for your podcast episodes which are optimized for Google search, as well as create videos optimized for YouTube off the back of it. Again, this will get you started quickly across all of the search-based platforms until you have the bandwidth to create original content for each platform. Creating and implementing the systems you need in order to create this bandwidth will be covered in Chapter 7.

Targeted Conversations

Have I ever told you about how Ash and I actually started dating? It's a pretty cringey story (we were 15 after all!), but well… it did the job! And we've been together ever since.

I had this image in my mind about how couples *should* get together. Boy asks Girl out, Girl says "Yes", Boy and Girl go on a date, have lots of fun and live happily ever after. And apart from the "go on a date and live happily ever after", our story didn't quite start this way.

Ash and I had liked each other on-and-off since 7th grade. However, by the time we were nearing the end of 9th grade, was Boy going to ask Girl out? it became more and more apparent that perhaps this wasn't going to happen.

So my friends and I decided that we had to take a hold (read: control) of this situation. And to give me the extra incentive or push, Maneesha made a deal with me. She would tell the guy she liked that she liked him, if I asked Ash if he liked me. Seemed like a fair deal (and honestly, I think I needed the accountability!)

Once the deal was made, Maneesha turned around in our math class and announced to Stephen that she liked him. Apart from the slightly shocked faces and giggles around us, I was surprised to find that the world did not fall apart around us.

I wasn't so sure that was going to be the case for my task, however.

Ash and I used to catch the same train together after school which is how we had become friends in the first place. And I knew that was when I had to do it.

As he was chatting away to me, relatively oblivious to my MOMENTOUS task, I could see the stations we were passing outside through the window as my own was getting nearer. I was going to have to get off soon, and I knew I wouldn't be able to face my friends (or myself) if I didn't do it.

My hands were getting clammy, my face was getting red and all I could hear was a ringing in my head. But I took a deep breath, turned to him and blurted out "doyoulikeme?"

There was a stunned pause and then he said…

"Yeah, why not?"

And that, my (potential future) kids, is how I met your father.

If there's one thing my parents instilled in me from a very young age, it's that "hope" is not the best strategy to get anything you want in life. And while I don't think they had wanted this lesson to be implemented in my teenage love life, it has always been how I try to operate.

If I had relied on hope for Ash to finally ask me out, would it have happened? Maybe. Maybe not. Who knows?

If I had relied on hope to get the grades I wanted, or the job I wanted, or move to the city I wanted, would any of it have happened? Again… who knows?

A lot of what we do as entrepreneurs is grounded in faith. We have to have faith in ourselves and our abilities to problem solve and take action. That's indisputable.

However, having faith and relying on hope are two different things. I have faith that I will live the life I was meant to live. Does that mean that I'm going to rely on hope to do that? No way!

I was not going to rely on hope to get my Dream Guy.

And I am certainly not going to rely on hope in my marketing to get leads - to get my Dreamiest Buyers - the lifeblood of my business. This is what I spoke to when talking about Passive Organic Marketing.

Whilst I am passionate about content creation and how important this is to build your credibility and connect with your audience, I am also very realistic about how limited it can be in actually generating your leads.

Because posting content after content on any social media platform and *hoping* that this is what will get you leads and build your business is *not* a good marketing strategy.

You have to be deliberate, intentional and strategic about how you get in front of your dreamiest buyers and bring them into your world.

This is where Targeted Conversations comes in.

Targeted Conversations is one of the most powerful ways for you to not only bring in leads, but also to hone in on your audience, marketing messages, and offers.

Remember Bernie Sander's mittens that blew up so much, the teacher who made them could not take any more orders? That could be you, without a random stroke of luck turning your product into a meme. Here, you will learn exactly how to make your offer take off with a strategy and the intention for growth. So… where do you begin?

We have already mastered our Passive Organic Marketing - this is important for you to build your authority and create that connection with your audience immediately when they inevitably land on your profile to check you out!

Doing this is going to get you your *qualified followers*.

And now? In this tier of The Traffic Pyramid, we are going to keep increasing your number of qualified followers AND start getting you *qualified leads* too!

Let me pause here for a second and discuss this key difference - between just getting *leads* and getting *qualified leads*. One of the reasons we strongly recommend doing this tier before investing thousands of dollars into paid ads is because Targeted Conversations will force you to know who your *qualified leads* actually are. Who are your dreamiest buyers who will be compelled with what you have? Because everyone else will either be pre-qualified out by you, or will choose to opt out on their own. Once you then turn the (hopefully successful!) ads tap on, you may expect to get a larger volume of leads more quickly, but I can guarantee that the quality will be a *lot* lower.

So let's get back to how we do Targeted Conversations. There are two ways: (1) Visibility Growth Hacking; and (2) Organic Outreach.

Let's start with Visibility Growth Hacking.

Visibility Growth Hacking

You may have guessed that my entire dating career (and that's really stretching it) has been confined to the antics and strategies of high-schoolers. So when I was trying to think of a way to explain Visibility Growth Hacking in a way that made sense... Well, that's where my mind went!

So let me lay it out for you - exactly what it is we're trying to achieve with Visibility Growth Hacking.

Do you remember your first high school crush? And how it felt to want to climb out of obscurity and become *known* to them? What did you do? Did you find yourself trying to get into the same assignment group as them? Did you perhaps spend your lunchtimes in the same vicinity as them? Did you manufacture excuses to "bump" into them?

When you were doing any and all of these things, you were essentially Visibility Growth Hacking. You were finding ways to become *visible* to them because we innately know that that's the first step to becoming known, and from there becoming liked, getting asked out on a date, being trusted and then having our happily ever after!

In the context of social media, Visibility Growth Hacking is all about coming back to a fundamental tenet of using social media platforms - to be social. What we want to be doing, very simply, is to do daily targeted engagement with our dreamiest buyers *and* our Dream 100 collaboration partners (more on this in the next tier!) so that we can start to become visible to them.

If we do not do this, we are missing out on a huge opportunity to leverage the number of people on social media platforms. This is a must-do for anyone looking to monetize their content on social media.

To begin, if we are on Instagram or TikTok, we are going to look at the hashtags they might be using, or looking through the followers of other businesses or accounts you believe they are currently congregating with. If you've chosen Facebook, you are going to find your audience by finding the groups that they would be members of.

And you are simply going to engage with them! The important thing to remember about this strategy is that you are not promoting, you are *participating*. You are participating in the conversations your dreamiest buyers and Dream 100 are having, you are being seen, becoming visible and you are helping yourself become known.

This is a great way to hack engagement for your own posts, to get visibility on your profile and ultimately what it is that you do. And all you are doing is being an active member of other people's communities. This is such a great, non-pressured yet active way to get yourself in front of *your* people.

If you happen to be having a fantastic conversation and would like to extend it *even further*, this is where direct messages come in a.k.a. Organic Outreach.

Organic Outreach

You now know my story about losing thousands of dollars jumping straight into running Facebook ads. Unfortunately, it's a very common story for new business owners. Which is why I cannot stress enough how important this tier of the traffic pyramid is. When you know your ideal buyer as you would a family member, you know their interests and behaviors, and you know how they talk about their pain point or their goals. That's when it's almost like you have your ad audience built and ad copy written for you!

I felt like a proud mother-hen after speaking to one of my clients recently. Bo Zhao started working with us to get help growing her baby gear rental business (like Rent the Runway but for baby gear).

I remember the slight frustration in her voice just before she joined our program. Like many new business owners, she knew she was onto something, but hadn't quite been able to get the traction she needed to validate this new business model.

She knew this was going to be the business that would be able to help mothers all around the world reduce the stress, money and waste that comes with buying and growing out of baby gear.

The problem was that while there were many women she had spoken to and sought feedback from previously saying "yes, love this idea!", "Yes, this is a great idea!", "the world totally needs this!" They weren't signing up. Even when she was offering it to them for free!

That left her wondering: was this really such a great idea? All these women are so generous with their time, and when given the opportunity to be a tester with no cost, they didn't take it? If that wasn't working, what else would?

She tested some other ways. She tried holding webinars, providing training about the things you really need as a new mom, with a lead in to her pitch. Still crickets. She even tried running some Black Friday holiday deals with a 50% off discount. Still nothing. She then tried running some ads which got her a lot of spam responses and one slightly legitimate one who turned out was just "bored" when she came across Bo's ad and wanted to tell her that it sounded like a great idea.

Nothing was working!

And Bo, who had an Ivy League MBA, was left wondering if maybe the business wasn't as great an idea as she thought… or that maybe it was just her. All she wanted to do was to help other moms out there with this problem that she struggled with, but no one was compelled in the same way to try it.

And then she joined our program, and now armed with the right outreach strategy, she joined more targeted Facebook groups. She wasn't limiting herself to the one Philadelphia Mom group she had been nurturing before. She started joining groups related to "sustainable living," "sustainable moms," "sustainable Philly," "evidence-based parenting," etc. She also started searching for her dreamiest buyers on Instagram.

Then she started having conversations and going through the "2 weeks of pain." It's the period of time that is super awkward and makes you feel self-conscious because you have no idea what you're doing at first. She literally would blurt out everything about her business in one message initially. Yes, it was painful and awkward. All the things you feel when you're learning something new. I remember speaking to her during those two weeks and I could sense the uncertainty. She'd ask me, "How long is this supposed to take? How much time am I supposed to spend on this? When will I see results?"

I knew that this was going to be the pivotal moment because this is the point when most people give up. They would rationalize it in other ways like, "Well my offer isn't worth a lot, should I be spending all this time trying to get these handful of sales in this way?" And then they'll just go back to doing things the "safe" way. But what they forget is that people buy from people first. They want to know who you are and what you stand for, especially if you haven't built up your brand yet. This was what Bo also realized. Because now she was having the right conversations with the right people.

Finally, we started getting bombarded (in a great way!) with daily posts and texts from her about a new sale she had and new customers started rolling in. It made a massive difference to her business. She was on a roll. She told me: "It feels awesome! It feels so natural now. It literally feels like a normal conversation I get to have to help someone."

The Art of Outreach

When reaching out to strangers, the last thing you'd want is to have an awkward undertone of copy/paste spam and that dreadful anti-personal "slime" that makes them roll their eyes and hit the delete button.

The first outreach is to initiate a real conversation with them, and find out what they'd be looking for help with in aspects relevant to your offer. Go for rapport. Think about how you could genuinely get to know the person and what makes them tick. The key word is *discovery*.

You reach out knowing your strategy, yet with a real desire to discover who's an appropriate fit for your tribe, email list, and offers. Awkward slime is allergic to authenticity. It loves when people have counter-intentions and are emotionally hung up on outcomes. So, steal the slime's nutrition: be authentic with your outreach, and talk to people as if you would in a cafe, or face-to-face at a networking event.

Also, respect your time, of course. That's where pre-qualification comes into play. You want to build your audience with people who are a right fit. Have a look at the profile of the person you're about to message and take stock. You don't have to creep on their life history. But find something that stands out to you as a conversation starter; something you could address. Move the conversation into the DMs. Thank them for connecting/accepting your friend/follow request. End your interactions with a question to help you get to know them better.

For example: "Hey, Abby! Thank you for accepting my friend request. I checked out your profile, and saw these beautiful dogs on your feed. What breed are they?"

Give a little bit of information about yourself by responding to their reply, and ask a question at the end, slowly transitioning into questions regarding your business niche. Have a natural conversation. If you're both comfortable, you could even send them voice notes or exchange pictures of common interests from time to time to establish a more personal bond. Sometimes, you message the wrong person, and that's okay too. It's better to realize you're barking up the wrong tree rather than waste time forcing a conversation. How do you figure that out? It's simple. You'll feel like you're pulling teeth… *"if it doesn't flow, let it go."*

I've noticed that people fear doing outreach because they don't want to be pushy. So, the other thing to keep in mind is that every interaction achieves *something,* and that does not have to be a direct sale.

Your next step could be a gift or an invitation: offer the person an invitation to your Lead Attracting Conversion Event (outlined in the next chapter), for instance. That's a great way to build your tribe, while also testing whether you have something compelling to offer. However, make sure that you tell them exactly why you're inviting them, with the benefits. Ask before you send the gift or invite, and drop the link only when they say "yes".

Most importantly, keep the conversation going and *give*. They'll know you're not a selfish and transactional individual but someone who genuinely displays interest. Who knows, you might even make a sale due to their curiosity and land the most loyal clients of your business (I sure did!). At the very least, you'll have made a new friend!

When Bo and I were talking about her Organic Outreach, she said she's now built her muscle memory. Each time she reaches out, she doesn't agonize over each response any more. She can now feel confident at any point because the whole point of her reaching out is to help other moms.

The Science of Tracking Your Lead Generation

We've spoken to the art of doing your Targeted Conversations. But as we know now, the *art* cannot be effective without the *science*.

If you recall, we went through the most important metrics to turn your passive social media content active - reach, engagement and the number of qualified followers. All of these culminate into the most important metric you want to be tracking with your organic lead generation: the number of qualified leads.

The number of qualified followers will drive the number of qualified leads because this is low-hanging fruit for you. When you have new followers, you should *always* be in their DM's thanking them for following you and building that rapport. They've already expressed an interest in what you do and have to say, why not see if they'd like to be kept in touch more formally by joining your email list, or even by joining your Lead Attracting Conversion Event?

We are rigorous with tracking our leads from social media. Every person that we contact is added to a CRM or spreadsheet and tracked through the particular touchpoints leading into a sale conversion. This is especially important to do once we get into systemization and delegation because I can tell you now… you do NOT want to be spending all your time doing Targeted Conversations! And yet, you need a system to stay on top of the data and metrics and be able to guide yourself and your team on the success of implementing this strategy.

Part of this tracking is also establishing a systemized approach to identify the common threads that weave into and tie your ideal buyers together. These common threads are an invaluable asset to have on hand when you start to build your paid ad campaigns.

They help you decide what audiences to build, what wording to use and how to position your offers. With our Targeted Conversations for our original coaching business, Bona and I started with the demographics of our dreamiest buyers and a broad need around solving their eCommerce sales issues. Women in late 20s early 30s, moms in late 20s to mid 30s, moms in late 30s to 40s and women who were partnered with no kids; all of whom owned an eCommerce business and needed a strategy to grow it.

As we had real conversations with real women in these broad categories, we were able to collect real stories and intel on the problems they were facing, the aspirations they were working towards, other interests they had and what they spent most of their time doing. And we wrote it all down, grouping together the common themes.

How they described their problems and aspirations helped us craft the words for our ads and what products or lead magnets we wanted to feature. Their various interests (e.g. home decor, yoga, Pilates, astrology, pets, plants, travel, literature) and what they spent time doing helped us build different audiences to target.

Getting this deep insight into your ideal buyers is the biggest gift from the hard work of doing Targeted Conversations. Because it will enable you to start scaling all that work quickly, easily and cost-effectively with paid advertising.

Running paid ads as a new business still requires a lot of testing and quite the learning curve, but starting with the foundation you've built from Targeted Conversations means you can shorten this learning curve.

Now that we know how to optimize performance of your Passive Organic Marketing, turning it into Active Organic Marketing, let's head over to the third tier of The Traffic Pyramid – Leveraging Other People's Audiences.

Tier 3: Leveraging Other People's Audiences

I knew just how good our desserts were. We had put so much effort into creating these divine creations and had so many taste-testing parties, that it was almost an impossibility to not be successful. When we opened The Choc Pot, I was expecting our doors to be beaten down. I was naive though. I believed our dishes alone were good enough to have people finding us and flooding the store. Two months into opening, reality struck. I had to get real about what we were doing because we were only making $100, maybe $200 a day. Some days went by only selling a handful of coffees! We were bleeding money because we had rent and wages to pay; we had supplier bills piling up!

The "build it and they will come" strategy was not working! It was one of the loneliest moments in my life, to the point where I started feeling claustrophobic being in the store. And I knew that I had to do something differently. I had to work out some way of getting the word out there. Because even through all of my doubts, uncertainty, crippling anxiety, and the feeling that for some reason, people just didn't like us – there was a fire inside me that knew we were onto something.

Fast forward a few weeks later, my husband and I had one of those very rare nights that we were both able to take a breather. At our dinner date we received a call from one of our *very frantic* team members, saying, "Guys you have to come in. I can't explain right now, I have to serve this drink. But we need help! You've gotta come in… Now!!" We couldn't help thinking "OMG! What's going on? Has something blown up? Have we lost power? What is it?"

So, we ran to the car, hopped in, and drove as quickly as we could (without running any red lights), trying not to freak out. When we got to the front of the store, I could still remember the sight before me. *The place was packed!*

We had a line of people waiting to get tables! We had people moving tables to create more space. Our poor team members were literally running back and forth from the kitchen to the tables serving people. It was chaos, but glorious chaos. It felt like we had become an overnight success.

What had we done that changed our downward spiral?

I had reached out to a bunch of different food bloggers and influencers. They were coming in, maybe one or two a week, for a few weeks. It's not like getting them to post or blog about us made us an immediate overnight success, but it was the momentum they were building. The more that people saw us, read about us, the more that they were like, "Okay, I have to try this place because *EVERYONE* is talking about them!"

And I had an "aha!" moment. The ONLY way we could build this type of momentum quickly is to leverage people with large audiences, where their audience is an ideal fit with ours!

Leveraging other people's audiences is super powerful for many reasons: it's incredibly effective to help you amplify your message *quickly*; it gets you more visibility and awareness; it gives your brand credibility; it helps you grow your own follower-base and email list; and it can help you fast-track sales growth.

It is also in the tier *before* Active Organic Marketing because with your time as a finite resource, you want to be putting it into a strategy where you can create as much leverage and visibility as possible.

Because of all of these reasons, I am a HUGE fan of this strategy. But only when it's done right with the requisite thought put into it.

I know it might be tempting to go out there and start to find all these people with large audiences to work with, but you need to consider who to work with, how to work with them, and ultimately, what is the outcome you are looking for?

What is your product/service/offer? Are you looking for direct sales? Are you looking to increase brand awareness and visibility? Are you looking to build your followers and/or email database?

Being clear on the direct outcome you are looking to achieve by leveraging someone else's audiences will make it easier to communicate, help them funnel their audience to the right place and ultimately, to track.

I got my first ever taste of leveraging other people's audience by working with **Influencers** almost a decade ago in the typical sense of how we might think about influencer marketing - individuals or accounts on any given platform who have a large number of followers (e.g., Instagram, Facebook, TikTok) or subscribers (e.g., a podcast, YouTube). When working with these types of influencers, keep in mind that they generally can't get *directly* in touch with their followers unless they pop up on their audience's Explore, Home or Stories feed, or the platform sends a notification about new content.

I have found Influencer Marketing incredibly effective for product-based businesses. However, not all Influencers are created equally, and like with all things in digital marketing, you will need to experiment with a few and see which ones work for you and your product and which ones don't before doubling down.

Dream 100 is a concept/strategy that I first heard about from Russell Brunson, and then implemented with the help of a mentor, Dana Derricks. Whilst Dream 100 can technically include the Influencers I've already mentioned above, I have separated them in my own mind and have instead given them the definition of people or businesses who typically have an email list that they can directly reach out to. Dream 100 has been an incredibly effective strategy as I have transitioned from product-based businesses into providing services, consulting and coaching.

Let's dive first into how we might work with Influencers if you have a product-based business.

Influencer Marketing

How could you reach 10,000 of your ideal customers? You could reach out individually, but that would take a lot of time. If you were sending 100 DM's per day, you could do that in less than a third of a year. Or, you could work with 5 influencers who each have 2,000 people as an audience and have it done by next Friday. See how that simplifies everything!?

Influencers have built their audience. If they've done it in the correct way, their audience trusts them, engages with their posts, and (most importantly) takes that action the influencer asks them to take.

Every time we launched a new store for The Choc Pot or Stax On Burgers (our burger restaurant), the first thing we did was to create an Influencer Pre-opening Party. We would invite dozens and dozens of social media Influencers to check out the new store and have some free food. It was the most effective way to get a ton of them taking photos, posting about us and creating a buzz!

This was an event we threw at the opening of our store in Chatswood, where we went all out creating games and prizes to keep them entertained as well:

Leveraging influencer's audiences is "win-win-win." The audience gets to know you and your products, giving them the opportunity to try something new. The influencer gets the social currency of being "in the know." And you get to add to your no. of qualified followers, email database or even make sales!

There are a variety of ways you could be working with influencers. One is that you can leverage them to directly sell your product to their audience. The influencer would promote your product and offer a special discount code available to their followers only. The influencer would get a % commission on each sale they make, the customer would get a discount, and you get a sale (plus a new email on your database)! It's a win-win-win.

The second way is collaborating with them with the intention of adding to your no. of qualified followers (and eventually your email list). The most effective way I have done this and seen this be done for any product-based business is through running a Like & Mention campaign on social media with them. You both add to your follower base and the winner gets a compelling prize comprising your products. Again, win-win-win!

Finding Your Influencers

The number one (and non-negotiable) characteristic of an Influencer you're looking to work with is that they have gathered a following of your dreamiest buyers. You can easily and quickly determine this by having a look at their individual follower profiles, from which you can make a pretty good determination about whether they are your ideal customers.

It's important to mention that when looking to work with Influencers on social media: there's a lifecycle. At first, we like to target "micro influencers" who are people with approx. 100K followers or fewer. We're looking for people who want to grow with us. Usually before the 100K level, the influencer is not necessarily looking for upfront payment for shout-outs or post shares.

Pay attention to the number of followers they have, and the engagement rates on their page. These days it's simple to buy followers, which ultimately flops, because you'll see 25K followers with barely 250 likes and annoying bot comments. You're looking for Influencers that have not only built a large following, but a genuine following. And just like how I spoke about the important metrics like *Engagement* for your own content, that is the same metric you want to be using to determine which Influencers you work with too.

You want to track down genuine influencers and build relationships with them. You do this by reaching out to them, building rapport and offering to send them a freebie sample package of your product or invite them to your cafe, like we did!

You may want to make it optional about whether they post about you straight off the bat. We've found it incredibly effective (if you can afford it), to give them free product without any expectations that they post about it. If they like your product, they'll post and rave about it even more because you're leaving it completely up to them to do so. It's like getting a genuine product testimonial, just pushed out to thousands and thousands of people!

Now that you've found them, how exactly do you work with them?

Working with Influencers

When we first leveraged influencer marketing for The Choc Pot, I have to admit that I didn't really know what I was doing. There was no real strategy to exactly who we were reaching out to and how we would be working with them. At the time, we were fortunate that as the platform was growing, people were organically growing with them, which meant that not only did they have a true follower base, but they also didn't have huge expectations or demands.

That isn't the case any longer. We now need to work with them in a way that not only adds value to ourselves, but also adds value to them and their followers. They've built an asset in their follower base, and it is in their best interest to protect it from content that is not relevant or of value.

When I was thinking about what more we could do with them for The Choc Pot, having worked with them for a period of time and seeing how they were working with other brands in retail and e-commerce, I started noticing a trend.

Giving them the ability to put their name to something - to collaborate with brands on something that was unique to them - gave them an opportunity to really promote something one-of-a-kind that was valuable to them and their followers.

And so, for The Choc Pot, we started collaborating with them on new desserts that they had direct input into. They would come up with the flavor combinations and perhaps a rough sketch or provide visual inspiration for what they were thinking, and we would bring it to life for them.

And they promoted the heck out of it!

Now, I am definitely not suggesting that you create new products with influencers (especially if you're just starting out), but how do you take that concept and apply it to something less labor-intensive and helps you build your traffic? How can you collaborate with them on a lead magnet? Perhaps a giveaway? A quiz? Be creative and have some fun with it! And definitely get their input! The more that they can co-create with you, the more bought-in they will become to actually promote you and the offer. You've made it irresistible for them!

As I've transitioned from product-based businesses to coaching and consulting, I've had to think differently about leveraging other people's audiences. I've had to expand the definition of "influencers" in my mind to *anyone* with a *network*. Meaning, they don't have to just be influencers on social media.

This is where Dream 100 comes in...

Dream 100 with Dana Derricks

I had been so used to leveraging other people's audiences in a certain way (i.e., through social media Influencers) that I had no idea where to start with the Dream 100 strategy. I understood the concept, but didn't quite know how to put it into practice.

That was when I first came across Dana Derricks who has cleverly carved this niche out as his own, including developing software that helps make this process so much easier! Dana's work with Dream 100 has been directly responsible for hundreds of millions in revenue for his clients and building multiple 7-figures businesses of his own in several different verticals.

I spoke to Dana about all things Dream 100 to share with you (by Dream 100'ing him!). The rest of this section on Dream 100 is in his own words:

I've been doing Dream 100 my whole life, even when I was a kid. I remember riding my bike around my neighborhood, recruiting my neighbors so we could all get high-speed internet because we needed to have 12 people signed up to qualify for it!

I started getting really serious about it when I was in my early 20s. I read a book called '*The Ultimate Sales Machine*' written by a guy called Chet Holmes. And in Chapter 6, he talked about this strategy called the Dream 100. At that moment, I realized: "Holy crap I've been doing that!"

I had been doing Dream 100 for everything! I finally had a name for it!

For my business, I was creating collaborations before I even knew what they were.

And I was definitely Dream 100-ing in my personal life. When I was a Senior in High School, I wanted to play college football, but it wasn't going to happen because I went to a really small school. I printed out a list of 40 different colleges and put together a package that had a highlight tape, a recommendation letter from my coach, etc. and I mailed it out to all 40 colleges.

Long story short, I ended up being recruited by half of them and received a scholarship that covered almost all of my tuition!

The Dream 100 Strategy

One of my mentors, Russell Brunson, wrote the foreword on my Dream 100 book and he's actually quoted on the cover saying "[Dream 100] is the foundation of our entire company…"

A lot of people think that the Dream 100 strategy is sending people stuff in the mail, or it's getting a collaboration, or it's finding affiliates. And it's not! It's actually *everything*…

It's creating a network of contractors. It's creating a list of potential acquisition targets. It's all of these things!

Which is why I think Dream 100 is the most important strategy you can employ.

That's why I get excited about it.

From a practical standpoint it's this… if you have a problem, your Dream 100 are the people that can and will solve it for you. As a strategy, Dream 100 is about creating a value exchange or a value-based relationship with them so that you can get the problem solved somehow.

Getting Started

To do Dream 100 effectively, you want to go after a mixture of what I call the A, B and C-level people of your niche.

You want to target a handful of A level people - the Oprah Winfrey of your world - to nurture over a long period of time. Yes, it will take a long time (years in fact) to build a proper relationship with them. Is it worth it? Oh yeah!

While you nurture your A level, your bread and butter are your B's and C's.

If we use baseball as an analogy, your A's are like your walk-off grand slams. This happens once a season and it's amazing!

Your B's are like your doubles and triples and home runs. They get you wins!

And your C's are the singles. They get you on base, which also contributes to your wins.

So that's how I focus my efforts - on B's and C's while nurturing my A's. You don't have to shoot for the moon right away!

The next thing is to start with who you already have a relationship with. Get them out of your head, out of your phone, out of your email and put them down on paper, in a spreadsheet or even better, in the Dream 100 software!

The list may not be very congruent, but there are already people there who can help solve a problem for you. And one of the worst mistakes that I see people make with Dream 100-ing is they don't ask people they already have a relationship with!

Imagine dating someone for 10 years and they're like the perfect person for you but you're too scared of them saying "No" so you don't ask them to marry you. Look at what you're potentially missing out on for the rest of your life! So, don't be afraid to ask.

The rule of thumb I use is if you don't think they're going to say "Yes" to what you ask them, give them more value. Just keep pushing value, to the point where you are certain that they are going to say "Yes" to whatever it is you're asking for.

I guarantee that for *everyone*, there IS someone who is ready to say "Yes" to you, no matter what that is. You've just gotta start taking advantage of that and you'll see how cool this process is and you'll want to go and do it more and more!

Here are some practical things you need to do when you start out and don't have a relationship with someone you're Dream 100-ing:

1. First up, consume as much of their stuff as you can. When you've done this, it will come across when you engage them, which will make them excited to actually talk to you! Does it mean you have to buy everything they have? No! Especially if you can't afford it. But you can listen to their podcast you can read their blog posts, you can buy their books, etc. It doesn't have to cost much money. If you don't have a ton of money, invest your time doing this.

2. Next, go into their community and provide value. One thing I did in one of my best Dream 100 relationships with Russell Brunson is I went into his ClickFunnels group, when it was still relatively early on and I just answered people's questions. I gave them value and I asked for nothing in return. People try to do that with a hidden agenda of trying to get them as a client, but I never did that. And very soon, I started being noticed by the leaders in that community.

3. Finally, become a customer. This applies to everybody, even for example, a YouTuber. If they have merchandise you can buy, then buy it! Buy their shirt. Because when you reach out to your Dream 100, the first thing that they'll do is look for them in their system. So, I always make sure that I'm a customer even before I try to build connections, because that way they can know who you are ahead of time. And you can't really ignore a customer! So, make sure you're a customer, even if it's just a book.

Declare Your Dream Outcome

When you want to build a Dream 100 relationship, you need to declare an outcome. This is something we were really intentional about building into the software - there's literally a field called "Dream Outcome". Type it in!

Because this is going to guide the *whole thing*.

No two paths will ever be the same. My path with Russell for example - my dream outcome is that I want him to acquire my company someday. That's my dream outcome.

And along the way, I've been able to speak at Funnel Hacking Live, I've been able to work with him privately in his office, I've been able to go to Boise and hang out with his kids. And that wouldn't have happened without me declaring my dream outcome. Because all of this had to happen in order for me to get closer to this dream outcome. And I know it sounds crazy! But declare it and just let the value exchange build until the dream outcome no longer seems crazy.

The Dream 100 Software

I created the Dream 100 Software because of a couple of problems I was facing.

If you think about a time you met somebody, whether it was at a conference or in passing, how many times did you get a business card only for it to end up in the laundry and then in the bin?

In all these different interactions you have - online or in-person - you build a really great connection and then it fizzles out. This is where a lot of people get stuck. They create these 'Barney' relationships where, like Barney, they go around hugging all these different people but then nothing really happens.

The next problem I specifically had is I wanted to get more organized and focused on this. So, I started putting people into spreadsheets and created scripts and saved them on Notepad, and tried to manage it all that way, which makes it super clunky! And not at all user-friendly and it is definitely not scalable!

That's where the Dream 100 software comes in. It's super easy to use, you can add people straight in there in a few clicks and you can organize it really easily. You can be really intentional with what your ideal outcome is that you want from that person. You also have a checklist so you can keep your team and yourself accountable to the tasks.

It also scrapes their social media posts so you can stay top-of-mind without having to annoy them. And there's scripts you can save straight into the software which in one click, copies them, and in another click, opens up a chat window or email composition window, so you can just copy and paste the script straight in.

It's everything you don't get when you manually Dream 100. The Dream 100 software gives you all the tools to make it happen faster and more easily.

The Most Important Metrics when Dream 100-ing

The results cycle with Dream 100 can be a little bit longer because you're building relationships. The main metric I keep track of is the *number of outbound messages sent a day* (including first touch and all of the follow ups). My Dream 100 Manager sent out 71 messages and I got a response rate of 15, which is huge!

It's one of those strategies that have a snowball effect. You keep pushing and pushing and pushing, and once you get over the hill, you'll probably have too many opportunities to keep up with!

Setting the specific target for the number of outbound messages depends on the campaign you're running. Right now, I'm aiming to get 200 people for my next campaign. 50 - 70 messages a day will get this filled right up!

Even if you do half of that - 10 messages a day - it is better than zero. Just get started!

My Top Tips for Dream 100'ing success:

- **Speak the language of your recipient.** Dream 100-ing does not mean "affiliates" to everybody. It may for some, but not for everybody. For example, let's say you have a supplement brand and you want Instagram influencers to promote it. What many people do wrong is they ask the Influencer "Hey do you want to be my affiliate? I'll give you this in commission." And the influencer will respond with "What's an affiliate? No." So in this example, speaking their language might sound like "Hey, I'd like to sponsor you. Can you give me your sponsorship packages?" 100% response rate! Because you're speaking their language. And eventually you want to ascend that relationship up into them becoming an affiliate. That's how I helped Lady Boss grow their Partner Program from zero to $1 million/month in 6 months!

- **Break down your A's, B's & C's**. The optimum spread for your Dream 100 is 10% A's, 30% B's and 60% C's.

- **Your Dream 100 doesn't always mean 100 people**. The number of people on your Dream 100 list depends on your situation. For example, if you're a local business in a small town, there's probably not 100 other businesses that can provide referrals, so maybe it's a dream 40. On the flip side, if you feel like there are a lot of people who could promote you, don't have a Dream 1000! Go deep, not wide. Stick to a Dream 200 for example.

- **Relentless follow up is what makes this work**. My Dream 100 Manager has been going crazy in my DM's! And there are some names in there that I don't even deserve responses from. It's crazy and overwhelming and trust me, I *still* get sick to my stomach when I send messages to people like that. So, it might not go away and that's ok. On the other hand, we can go through four separate follow ups with no responses.

- **Don't put any conditions on this.** Don't *expect* a response. If they don't respond, it doesn't say anything about you. It doesn't mean they're a jerk. And that doesn't necessarily mean that you're annoying them or that they're not interested. It just means they're busy!

The Future of Dream 100-ing

We're going to get back to more relationship-based marketing and integration marketing, which is all about Dream 100-ing!

The days of being able to run Facebook and TikTok ads and being able to strike it rich are gone. Getting people's attention and trust is harder than it's ever been and to have that built-in credibility of a strategic partner who is promoting you and *prescribing* you - as opposed to you coming across as a cold ad to somebody - is the way to go!

And in order to have someone prescribe you? Just *give*! Give so much value they can't say "No".

For example, most people join a coaching program or a course and don't get a result. That's just the math.

I *choose* to get an ROI no matter what! It doesn't matter about what content I bought or what I thought I was going to get. It's in the *relationships* I build within that community.

For example, when I joined Russell Brunson's Inner Circle, I sent a one-way wire for $25,000 and for the first 4 months I thought I had been scammed! I got nothing out of it, I didn't get any courses or anything! And then I went out to his Mastermind event at his office with 30 other people in the group and I immediately knew that this was where the value and the ROI was.

I see this in myself and in others all the time. Sometimes the reason why we may have joined something isn't actually what we get out of it. It actually ends up being something better!

So, lead with value and you *will* get an ROI!

If you want to know more about Dream 100 and test drive Dana's Dream 100 software, I've included a direct link at www.deirdretshien.com/resources.

I am a big believer in following and modeling what works. Before meeting Dana, I had much more of a scarcity mindset. I used to (irrationally) think that there weren't enough of my people out there, and that *all these people* were my competition, and that I couldn't "give away" all of my knowledge and tactics and secrets.

Ever since being in Dana's world and seeing the amount of value he provides and how much he gives away, I have been inspired. Because I know first-hand being a buyer of his that his willingness to provide value is why I want to work with him.

As a result, I give away so much more to my audience, to you (case in point: my exact strategy, which I've completely laid out in this book).

And now when I talk to my Dream 100, I don't hold anything back. I'm happy to give it all away to them so that, to Dana's point, they can integrate my stuff in with theirs and we can all grow together.

Following Dana's advice has already led me to build multiple relationships that I had never even dreamed I would be able to create, with Dream 100 people who have hundreds of thousands of people in their audience and list. People who my Dream 100 are now also helping me reach!

It isn't necessarily a strategy that is going to get you a super quick hit, because as Dana mentioned, it is *all* about relationship building. But it is one of the best strategies that will help you build a sustainable business. I will always be leveraging this strategy to build any business upon, and so should you!

I also know how daunting it might sound… to reach out to your Dream 100. Trust me, as an introvert this is the last thing I ever wanted to be doing! So, I'll let you in on a secret I used myself when getting started…

It's Already A "No"

The first time I ever ran a virtual summit, the thought of approaching potential guests for it - people who *didn't know me* - was terrifying!

Russell Brunson had told us to run a virtual summit because it's one of the best ways to build a relationship with your Dream 100. And even though I was all-in on doing it, and had prepared everything else to a tee, I was procrastinating on the most important piece - actually contacting the potential guest speakers!

Because deep-down, we don't want to be rejected, right? And that rejection is real when you're doing something like this, reaching out to complete strangers because as we all know - of course not everyone is going to want to work with you! Just like with everything else, this is all just a numbers game.

The fear is exactly what I felt when I decided to put together that first Virtual Summit. I wanted to pull together something so amazing, that brought together multiple experts talking on some really important topics because I wanted to provide a LOT of value for my audience. And ideally, I wanted to get at *least* 20 speakers.

But it was incredibly scary to send that first message and that first email. I spoke to a coach in Russell's team, Steve Batetzko, about it and he just looked at me. He does this thing where he goes silent for a second and he's either going to say something funny or something... not funny.

This time, it was on the not funny side. He looked at me for a second and he said "Deirdre. When you reach out to them, what is the worst they could say?"

And I was like... "I guess the worst they can say is "no"?"

"Exactly. Right now, having not reached out to any of them, is it a "yes" or a "no"?"

And of course, I said it was a "no".

"Right. it's already a "no". If they say "no", it's still a "no". So, what's the worst that could happen?"

And of course, my mind was just blown at the absolute simplicity of this. It was exactly what I needed to hear!

So, if you're feeling scared. If you're feeling like no one is going to want to work with you, that you're just this small business, that you're a "nobody" Then first of all, know that none of that is true regardless of the outcome. And second, come back to this point. It's already a "no".

By the way, my aim was to be able to hit 20 speakers, and I ended up with 32 amazing speakers who I have been able to build and continue a relationship with! I've also gone on to be on their podcasts, their virtual summits and have done joint lives with some of them to their audience - all of these great things to promote my business that would not have happened if I had sat in my fear and never reached out.

So always think "It's already a 'No'."

It's important that we remove this fear, this won't be the only fear we'll have to battle with in The Traffic Pyramid, especially as we start scaling into Paid Ads.

Tier 4: Scaling with Paid Ads

"I'm scared to try ads." "I ran ads but didn't get any results. What did I do wrong?" "My ads were doing so well. And then, they weren't. What happened?"

These are the most common questions and comments I get from clients when it comes to paid advertising. Chances are you're also in one of these buckets. The bad news? There's no silver bullet when it comes to ads. (And don't believe anyone who tells you there is!) The good news? Anyone can run ads successfully with the right mindset and approach.

The Ads Mindset

The biggest mistake people make when running ads is expecting sales straight away. Whether you're just starting out with new ads or optimizing ad campaigns that are already running, you have to remember that most customers have to see an ad at least 5 to 7 times before opting in. With our feeds as saturated as they are, it's more like 12 times that someone needs to be exposed to your offer before they opt in. Unless that buyer is already solution-aware.

Paid ads, especially early on, are an investment to collect data on what works and doesn't work with your dreamiest buyers. Yes, eventually, you'll have a well-oiled machine that will get you at least $4 back for every $1 you put in. But it takes time and work to get there. When I started running paid ads for our coaching business, I *still* fell into this mindset trap. Even though I had worked on so many client ads accounts before and I coached my clients on this mindset, I somehow still expected things to be different for me and to start converting on auto-pilot straight away.

I remember feeling frustrated and disappointed about not getting *results*. And then I realized I had a very narrow definition of results. I was fixating on immediate sales from a completely cold audience instead of focusing on what the data was telling me so I could refine my ads to warm the audience and *then* convert them. Once I shifted this focus to a test-learn-tweak approach, I got the results and sales I had wanted.

The Ads Approach

So, what do I mean by a test-learn-tweak approach?

Test: It's all about starting with a set of creative elements (images, videos), ad copy, offer and testing each combination with your target audiences.

Learn: Then you look at your metrics and analyze what the data is telling you. Which creative elements are working really well? Are your images and videos not stopping the scroll? Is your ad copy enticing customers to click through to your website? Which of your audiences are taking action?

Tweak: Based on what you've learned, make changes to your ad campaigns.

Businesses that are new to paid ads (especially) require a lot of testing, and the process is *quite* the learning curve. But starting with the foundation you've built from your Active Organic Marketing and the insights it gives you on your dreamiest buyer means you can drastically shorten this learning curve.

And even when you have your well-oiled ads machine, you can't set and forget. You need to keep experimenting with your creative elements, how you target your audience, the words you use and the offers you make.

This reminds me of one of my clients who had been running paid ads for years. They had enjoyed a regular return on ad spend of 3.2 (which means they were earning $3.20 for every $1 they were spending) but it was starting to inch down.

I reviewed their ads manager and realized their target audiences were tapped out and they hadn't created new imagery or ad copy let alone tested it.

Because I had already worked with them on their Traffic Pyramid – helping them makeover their social media for Passive Organic Marketing, collaborating with selected influencers to leverage their audiences and building a small but loyal community of raving fans from Active Organic Marketing – I had a rich base to dip into.

I collated the user-generated content that their customers and influencer partners had shared and used it as my ad creatives. I created new target audiences based on the other interests their community of fans frequently shared about. I wrote ad copy in the same vein as the organic conversations they were having with their customers.

I tested. I learned. I tweaked. I repeated.

And the results spoke for themselves. Their return on ad spend went from 3.2 to 7.8 in 3 months.

Tracking Your Ads Success

Once you have established your social media platform and start pushing content that attracts traffic while giving you sales, you know that you have meticulously followed each step on the ladder. However, your journey doesn't end there; this is just the beginning. Your traffic generation, sales and scaling up are all intertwined for the rest of the life of your business, because these are the threads of its fate. How do you know you're making progress and improvements organically, by involving influencers, with paid ads, and using other methods? You have to have something that shows you figures to keep stock of. Yes, tracking your success is an essential step that you will be doing regularly to keep a check on your growth rate, expenses to growth ratio and many more metrics.

For your paid ads, use the tools on your social media's marketing dashboard or ads manager console to check out metrics that show you:

1) **Purchases or Conversions:** This belongs right at the top of your list. Because everything else is just a vanity metric if your ads and landing pages aren't resulting in the number of sales or opt-ins you're aiming for.

2) **Cost Per Result:** How much is each *result* that you have set your ad up for (whether that is a click or a sign-up or a purchase) costing you? This will help you understand your current cost of a lead or conversion.

3) **Click-Through Rate (CTR):** Of people who see the ads, what % are clicking through to take the next step (whether that is to your landing page or other linked pages)? This will help you understand how effective your ad copy is at compelling your audience to click through.

4) **Engagement:** How is your audience interacting with your ad? Are they clicking on the link, sharing, liking, saving or reacting to the post? This will help you understand how much social proof your ad has.

5) **Reach:** Reach shows you how many people see your ads in a timeline.

6) **Impressions:** Impressions show you how many times your ad was viewed. Multiple views by the same account counts as an impression but not as a reach.

7) **Clicks:** Clicks refers to people clicking on your CTA that you mention.

To know which of these metrics work for you, you'll need to make your own benchmarks, with the help of:

- The industrial average benchmarks
- The economics of your brand
- The historical growth of your business

Once you see the shifts on different ads, lead magnets and organic growth techniques, you'll be able to chart out your "keep doing more of this" and "never doing this again" methods.

6.
LEADING YOUR TRIBE INTO THE SALE

Sometimes I love playing the "remember when…" game. It always takes me back to that different time in my life in high school, when things felt simpler.

I have so many memories I cherish; the piggy back races, the mini-soccer tournaments, the pranks, the laughter. I remember the sun on my face as we were lazing on the hill at lunch-time.

I've already told the story of a particular moment I cherish - how my now-husband and I "got together."

Kinda cringey, right?

But it got the job done and we've been together ever since!

So just the other night, Ash and I were playing the "remember when…" game. I was asking him about how he knew he liked me back in 7th grade and when it had happened. And he was telling me about the great legs I had. Typical male.

Then, he started telling me about this dream that he had one night where he was walking down some rocks towards a beach, being drawn towards a girl. And when she turned around, it was me. And that was when he *really* noticed me in high school and started liking me. Because I had infiltrated his subconscious.

Now the reason why I wanted to tell you this is because this is how marketing essentially works.

Every relationship, no matter if it is a romantic one, a platonic one, one between a brand and its customer, a service-provider and their client… always starts with something that magnetizes them together; something that "hooks" them in.

For our relationship, it seemed to be my legs. I knew I was drawn to him because of his ease of playing sports. All completely superficial. But once you're drawn in, even without knowing it, the subconscious takes over. And it is then our job to make something happen! So, I wanted to start with helping you work out your business's equivalent of my legs.

In this section, we're going to explore ways to move your dreamiest buyers from cold to converted. We'll create a Lead Attracting Conversion Event (LACE) that is going to draw your buyer in so that you start to infiltrate their subconscious. We'll then use *that same* conversion event to get in front of them so that the only thing they can say to you when you ask them to buy is… "Yeah. Why not?"

What are Lead Attracting Conversion Events?

When my mother announced to me that I was going to start extra lessons on Saturdays, she was really quite excited about it. I had recently taken a test and managed to secure a spot at a tutoring college for young gifted and talented students. She was confident that this was going to set me up for academic success.

Even though I didn't enjoy giving up my Saturdays as a third-grader, I was happy with how proud my parents were. I didn't know what to expect going into it except that doing these extra classes was meant to help with getting into the 5th grade Opportunity Class in school, and then ultimately into a Selective High School for 7th grade. Ideally the best one - the one that tops the equivalent of SATs every single year - James Ruse Agricultural High School.

So, I showed up every Saturday and did what I was told to do. It was honestly quite a lot of the same style of questions, centered around math and English. And throughout my time there, I was taking test after test, advancing into classes like the one called "Galileo's Gang" where I got to solve (actually pretty fun) puzzles.

At the time, there didn't seem to be much rhyme or reason to what I was doing and how I was doing it. I just showed up and did what I was told.

Looking back now, with the benefit of hindsight and (a little bit more) wisdom, I can see the simplicity of what was happening.

It was just repetition.

Were we learning totally different subjects than everyone else in school? Nope!

Were we learning any great new skills? Nope!

We were just showing up one extra day a week and pretty much doing the same thing over and over again.

In each class, we would keep doing the type of multiple-choice tests they would be giving us in the Selective School test. And our teachers would just give us a bit of guidance and feedback on how to tweak our approach slightly for the exam, and then we would do it again. And again.

We already had the capability - getting tutored was just putting discipline and focus around it.

Discipline and focus to actually *do it*. To implement everything we'd been learning and practicing. Over and over again.

And it worked!

Whatever class or school or grades my parents wanted me to get, I got.

Fifth grade Opportunity Class at Matthew Pearce Primary School? Check.

Seventh grade High School at James Ruse Agricultural High School? Check.

Scoring in the 99th percentile in the Twelfth grade High School Certificate (equivalent to SATs)? Check.

Since then, without even really realizing it, I've always sought mentors who can help me in whatever I've wanted to excel in. I've had tutors throughout high school, I've had mentors in University, in my corporate career and of course, in entrepreneurship.

It has been a constant in my life. People who can give me the overall strategy, provide feedback on how I'm implementing it and ensure that I repeat. And repeat.

Excelling at anything is all about repetition.

If I'm going to be honest, I was never the most naturally gifted at anything. I was certainly capable, just like we ALL are, but it is this repetition that has really propelled me forward into great things.

When I made the transition from a bricks & mortar business to online businesses, I knew straight away that I would not be able to do it alone. I needed mentors. I wanted to ensure that I had exactly the right strategies to convert people online. And the only way I knew how to shortcut my learning was to invest. Just like how my parents had always done with me from a young age.

So, I went about searching and finding multiple mentors that could help me with an online conversion strategy. They would give me feedback and guidance on how I've been implementing the strategy, and then repeating it.

And all of these mentors had built (or were currently building) well over 7-figure businesses - I invested in programs learning from people like Melissa Ricker, Dana Derricks and Josh Elledge, all the way to multi-millionaire and billionaire giants like Russell Brunson and Tony Robbins.

And in everything they've helped me implement, I've come to see a few commonalities, which I have conveniently summarized into a vehicle I call Lead Attracting Conversion Events, or LACE for short.

Now, why have I given it such a cumbersome name you might ask?

Because it was the only way I could encompass the power of these conversion events. Being able to not only attract and magnetize people, but to also convert at the *same time*.

And as Sloth Bosses, what better way to be efficient and effective with our time, then to have ONE event that does *both things*!

So, let me get into the three biggest commonalities - the must-haves - that I have learnt from my millionaire mentors about how to use this vehicle to sell online!

Magnetize Your Dreamiest Buyer

The first must-have for your LACE is that it has to be magnetizing… *for your dreamiest buyer*!

It sounds like a no-brainer but you'd be surprised at just how hard this is! Because there are two parts to this step, and most people only focus on one, if any at all.

Imagine you were following the Traffic Pyramid (as I know you have) and you are now doing your Active Organic Marketing. You want to be putting yourself in the best position to have awesome conversations and then *feel really good* about the thing you're going to offer them.

I know many people reading this book are heart-centered entrepreneurs like me and know what I mean when I say "feel really good" about it. Because a lot of times we create some type of lead magnet that we *think* will hook people because it may have worked for others, but it doesn't feel quite aligned with our brand or what we're here to do.

For me, for example, I had created a lead magnet around how to create an Instagram Reel - which seemed to be working for other people, and don't get me wrong, it is important to know if you want to grow your visibility on Instagram - but it didn't quite sit right with me.

So how do we feel really good about what we're attracting our dreamiest buyers with? We want to be solving a BIG problem to help them lift from their pain point or provide an amazing opportunity for them to increase their status and authority.

Every type of conversion event that my mentors have taught me have done one of these two things. For example, running challenges and hosting webinars are designed to solve a BIG problem for my dreamiest buyers. Running a Viral Contest or creating a podcast sales system are designed to provide an opportunity for my dreamiest buyers to increase their status.

I will be laying out the strategy for each of these types of conversion events (in my mentors' own words!) so that you can get a better idea of what may work best for your dreamiest buyer. You always just want to start with one type and make a good amount of money *with just that* before trying to add on another and another (trust me, I've tried it and overcomplication does NOT get you more sales!).

This is all about getting you disciplined and focused on implementing the one thing, and then repeating it.

So, we must first make our LACE magnetizing through solving a big problem or by providing an amazing opportunity.

The second part to this – which many miss – is that it has to be magnetizing to one specific person. And one specific person only. Not you, not your coach, not your next-door neighbor. But your dreamiest buyer!

This is something that I recently learnt from one of my mentors, Melissa Ricker. We were at a Mastermind Event at her beautiful home in Texas and she was talking about "Level 10 Clients".

What is a Level 10 Client? It is the client that you absolutely want to be serving, who will value what you do enough to pay for it, or find the means to pay for it. Who will show up for themselves and put in the work? Who might potentially already be at a certain level from a mindset and drive perspective?

When Melissa was talking about Level 10 Clients, I realized that this was the reason why some of our messaging or lead magnets weren't working, why we seemed to be attracting the wrong people. People who didn't value what we had to offer enough, or who didn't show up and put in the work.

Because while we *thought* we had honed in on our potential client, the level at which we had positioned our messaging was speaking to and attracting more Level 1 Clients who were still on their own journey of figuring this out for themselves, *not* our Level 10 Client.

For example, rather than promoting a lead magnet around how to create Instagram Reels, which speaks to a very beginner-level type of entrepreneur, how about creating a lead magnet around the metrics you need to keep your Virtual Assistant accountable to for Instagram? One was more advanced, and talked to a completely different type of person than the other - it talked to our dreamiest buyer.

Once we made this shift to talk to our Level 10 Client (and of course, run Messagelytics to test our hooks!), we started to bring in more of the right people. This is why it is so important to be magnetizing that one specific person!

But of course, this is just the start. Getting them into your world is just the beginning, because then you need to build that relationship with them.

Which leads me to the second must-have.

Create Human Connection

The second must-have for your LACE goes back to the same principles I've already spoken about with Content Trust Accelerators - stories, emotions and practical value.

And why is that? Because these three pillars are essential to creating human connection.

Human connection is at the heart of all sales. That became blatantly obvious through an experience with my second business called Stax On

Burgers. We had a crazy idea: what if we could recreate a food-truck burger experience, but do it indoors?

It was just the seed of a concept that took root and grew into something we thought could become great. We created a concrete indoor space with a truck-like facade. We also created new innovations in the ordering process. Customers were able to do all of their ordering via a kiosk, custom-design their burger, select their sides, and hang out in the novelty of the interesting ambience we created. Apart from McDonald's, no one else had that kind of automated system.

After weeks of going back and forth with a technology partner to create the system (trying to make the experience really cool) we finally opened our doors. When we did, I felt like a giddy child, bobbing up and down excited to see people use the system. I had to hold myself back from stepping in and pressing the touchscreen buttons for our customers. I was just so excited!

We were getting great feedback on the food. The burgers, the sides, the drinks were all on point. We could hear the satisfying sizzle of the meat on the grill, the refreshing cans of Coke popping open and the mouth-watering smell of tater tots cooking in the deep fryers.

We were growing, but then our sales flatlined and we didn't understand why. What was happening?

We brainstormed all the potential root causes of this problem we could think of. Was it the recipes for the burgers? Maybe there was new competition in the area? Was our social media not getting as much exposure? Maybe we just needed to do more pictures, or videos to keep people interested. Reviews?

We scrambled trying to find the hole so we could plug it up and continue growing. Then we noticed that most of the people who were coming in were mainly new customers. We weren't getting our existing customers to come back to us. While they were giving us great feedback when they came the first time, they just weren't coming back.

That's when I remembered what my mentor had said. "People may come into your business because of a product, but they stay because of their relationship with you".

As a result of our new kiosk, we had unknowingly completely removed the relationship-building aspect from our business. It was such a lightbulb moment for us. So, back to the drawing board.

We replaced the kiosk with a real person taking orders, building rapport, getting to know the customers. We tested making it a priority to show up for them. Guess what? Sales went straight back up again! We had customers returning to us.

That made me realize something else. In order to keep them coming back, you need human connection!

In other words: you need to show up for them. This applies to the online space even more than it does with brick-and-mortar businesses. The emotional connection with people online is so much less than live. We're in our own bubbles where people are reduced to little square icons and 140-character limit bios. That's hardly an ideal situation to build lasting rapport.

Unless you're a big brand like McDonald's, don't hide behind your social media, behind an ordering kiosk, or behind your online store. You have to show up for your audience and be visible. Engage with them. Do it in a meaningful way. Be present with them in real time. That's what they secretly want. They want to be heard. They want to feel a connection.

And you build this connection through sharing your stories and by giving a TON of value! If you can do this and help them feel something - evoke those emotions - then they'll want to share, they'll want to show up and they'll want to follow you!

Lead Them to The Sale

Which then leads me to the third must-have of your LACE... because where will your tribe be following you to? Where will you be leading them?

You'll be leading them to buy!

This is where the conversion component comes in. You've attracted them with something really compelling - either to solve a big problem they have, or to provide them with an opportunity to increase their status. You've connected with them, built a relationship because you have built an immense amount of rapport and shared with them through your stories.

And now, you don't want to leave your dreamiest buyers stuck. They are stuck and can't do it alone, because if they could then they wouldn't be following you right now, consuming your content. There's a reason why they were attracted to you with your LACE.

And so, it is your job to lead them. It is your job to step up and be their leader. Which means asking them to buy! That is the only way you can really serve them. Because your time and energy are not a free renewable resource. Your dreamiest buyers should be expecting to buy, because you will be helping to pave the way for them. That's what leadership is.

And leadership is also about helping people do things they weren't sure they were capable of doing before. All throughout my life, with all of the mentors, coaches, tutors I've had - the reason why I've been able to excel at anything I put my mind to is because they helped me see that I was capable of doing it.

And I was! They laid out the strategy, paved the way for me, gave me guidance as I stumbled along it and I just repeated and repeated.

And I come out the other end as a totally different person! Because of their leadership.

This is the impact you can also have on your dreamiest buyers. This is what entrepreneurship is all about. And it doesn't matter if you're thinking "I just sell clothes", or "I just sell nail polish", all the way up to "I coach people on transforming their marriages, transforming their lives".

No matter how big or small we think our impact is, we are still having an impact. It is with this impact that you are going to lead your dreamiest buyers into the sale.

While I have personally implemented these conversion events, and done them over and over again, I believe that I would be doing you and my mentors a disservice by trying to single-handedly teach you about them.

So, what I have done instead is I have interviewed some of my mentors for you, and have included these interviews over the next few sections so that you will be able to learn directly from them about the different conversion events, just like I did.

Let's start with one of the first online conversion events I learnt - The Live Launch Funnel (aka *The Challenge Funnel*).

The Live Launch Funnel with Melissa Ricker from Engineered to Scale

When we decided to transition into offering a coaching program with The Growth Boss, we didn't have a clue on where to start. We had a Facebook Group, but no real plan, no real strategy on how we were going to get our first clients. That's when we stumbled across Melissa and took a bootcamp that she was holding.

There was so much energy in her bootcamp and I could tell just how intelligent and data-driven she was. I instantly "vibed" with her. I knew she was someone who could help take me so much closer to where I wanted to be.

And so, when she made her pitch, I decided to make the investment in myself. And I haven't looked back since.

I launched my challenge 4 weeks after signing up (a MAMMOTH effort!) and unfortunately... got a big fat goose egg of sales, zero! She helped me dial it in and I launched again 4 weeks after. We got 2 sign ups! Not quite the 5-figure launch yet, but it was so exciting to see us trending upwards! I launched again another 4 weeks later and we finally hit 5-figures! And ever since, we've been consistently able to hit the 5-figure + mark.

What is the Live Launch Funnel? Fundamentally, it is a strategy where you are teaching your dreamiest buyers something over multiple days and then inviting them to take the next step with you. This could be buying into a course or program (if you're a coach), it could be to book a call with you (if you're a service-based business). It could also be to buy a product (if you're in e-commerce). In fact, we had an e-commerce client do over $20k in one week with this Live Launch Funnel selling their hot chocolate making machine and chocolates!

Here's how it works:

1. You decide what you want to teach about (depending on what your offer is) and work out how many days you need to teach that over (typically between 3 and 30 days).

2. Promote the event and have people register for it (following the Traffic Pyramid has been a game-changer for us here!)

3. Hold the event and towards the end of it (usually the second last day), make your pitch for your audience to take the next step with you.

When I decided to include this chapter about LACE, it was a complete no-brainer for me to invite Melissa to write about her Live Launch strategy. Here are her words:

I'm a nuclear engineer by degree and I worked in the corporate world for 10 years. At the time, I was climbing the corporate ladder. It was my obsession, I wanted to be the CEO of the company I was working for!

But then, I had my first baby and everything changed for me because I was working long hours and had a long commute. This was totally fine before but after having my son, I realized that someone else was raising my child.

I would wake up before he did in the morning and by the time I got home, he was already entering the crabby, grumpy phase. It just wasn't working and when he was 9 months old, I realized that this wasn't how I wanted my life to be.

And so, I up and left. I left a hefty paycheck behind. I knew I was smart and capable, so of course I could launch and run my own business!

Well turns out I had no idea!

I went from a high-flying manager to googling "how to make money from home".

I tried all sorts of different things. You name it, I probably tried it. Nothing was working, probably for a good couple of years. So, for 2 years, I wasn't making any money.

I was so fed up that I started getting ready to go back to corporate. I just couldn't do this anymore. I felt like such a failure!

But I decided to give it one more go. I revamped and started over with everything.

One of the bajillion different things I was trying was affiliate marketing. And I ended up winning a top affiliate award for ClickFunnels.

They flew me out to mastermind with Russell Brunson (mind you I was still not making very much money!)

And I asked him… "What's the biggest difference between those who get the Two Comma Club Award (from making a million dollars through one funnel) and those who don't?"

He asked me, "Well, if I open up your ClickFunnels account, how many funnels am I going to see in there? If I see hundreds of funnels, you're probably not. If I just see one or two funnels in there and you've been at it for a while, then you have a chance. Because it means that you're focusing and you're going all in."

I was thinking "Please don't open my ClickFunnels!" Because I had hundreds of funnels! And that led to my follow up question, which was "What funnel then? What funnel will help me hit the Two Comma Club?"

And he told me to focus on a high-ticket presentation funnel.

That was in August of 2019. I left that mastermind and spent the next 30 days wrapping my head around what that could look like for me. I love to teach; I love to talk and so I decided to do a challenge!

I had an offer at the end that I was selling for $3,000. I had never sold anything like that! But it was exciting!

So, I ran the challenge the first time in October of 2019 and… it kinda flopped!

But then I ran it again late 2019 and I got people to sign up! I had my first big $10k month!

I couldn't help thinking, "Wow ok… there's something here!"

The first time I launched my Challenge, my offer was literally "let me help you build a funnel" because that's what I knew how to do.

But then I started learning that a funnel was so much more than the tech! I had to really learn what it is my target clients wanted, what they got stuck on…They needed an offer, and they needed messaging.

And so, I launched in January 2020 again with a more comprehensive offer and out of nowhere I had a 6-figure launch.

So, December of 2019 I had made $10k and in January of 2020, a 6-figure launch!

It was crazy! And so, I launched it again and again and again and by August of 2020, I had over 7-figures cash collected, as well as multiple 7-figures of sales still coming in.

It was all a whirlwind but what it's taught me is that launching is super effective.

Why Live Launches are Exciting

The energy! The ability to give so much for free, build real momentum and make real progress during the week!

Live challenges completely flipped my mind around about sales. Because doing sales no longer feels slimy or sleazy or like a bait-and-switch.

That's why I love the challenge model. You can give so much and the selling part is just extending an invitation to your leads to keep going with something they already started. They're already pumped up and excited about it, and they're now invited to bring it full circle with you.

Live launches give entrepreneurs an ability to create this huge brand recognition and huge reciprocity in the market because you are able to give so much. And then the ability to grow your list with a path to the sale built into it!

It's not a lead magnet that then just takes forever to nurture and nurture for months and months. It helps you cast a wide net, give immediate value and it has a built-in way to make revenue. So, it's very effective and very fast.

Within a few days, you give people what they need to know to make a buying decision, and that's pretty incredible!

The Live Launch Strategy

I've learnt a lot about what makes an effective launch and I love to start with the thing you're actually going to sell and who you're going to actually sell to, so you can reverse engineer the content.

I call the launch the dressing room, where people can come in and "try you on" before they make the buying decision. So, we always want to start with the offer before we strategically ensure that the launch builds up to the offer.

Because when you transition your leads from your free (or even small paid challenge) to your paid offer, I want everyone to be able to say "I gave you this, but this isn't what you really want. Ultimately, this is what you want. And I'm extending an invitation to those of you who are ready and have this head start, but know there is so much more you have to do."

You have to start with the end in mind, so that when you give something to them for free, it makes sense and they can connect the dots between what you've already done and what is still left to go.

This opens their eyes and gives them the mindset shift they need so that what you're offering makes so much sense for them to continue with. This isn't just some lead magnet, a PDF or a download. This is actually a path to the sale. And so, you have to make sure that each piece of your live launch is actually building up to the end offer.

The Most Important Components of a Live Launch

You want to get really clear on the client that you ultimately want to work with on the backend, so that you can get more of them in and talk specifically to them, almost to the point that they feel like you've got a security camera watching them!

Being able to talk about their problems and fears and being better able to articulate it than they can… that's when you can really blow up your conversions on the back-end.

That's why I love live versus pre-recorded because you can actually see what's coming up for people. Yes, you want the bones of the content to stay the same because you're building an asset, but doing it live gives you the ability to adapt and see where people are so that you can meet them there.

One of the things I'll point out is that you have to get out of the trenches to figure this stuff out! So, while I love getting prepared as possible on the back-end, you have to put something out there, get people in, hear what they're saying to even understand what it is that they mean and want.

So, if you've never done a Live Launch before and you're not even understanding what a lot of this means, just go do it. Go do it and people will tell you what you need to know to perfect it going forward. It was my third time launching it before it really took off. I had to get it out there and see how people were responding and thinking about certain things.

When you think about your ideal client, you want to think about who actually gets results with what you teach, because it's not everybody! There's a million different people who teach launches in a very specific way, and there's a very specific person that gets results with me versus someone else.

I always like to think about, if you've worked with clients and you could replicate them a hundred times and that would make you incredibly happy and make your job so easy, what would they look like?

If you don't have that person yet, just think about… if you could create someone, how would they think and feel, how would they work? For me, I'm all about ambitious people. People who just get out there and do the work, people who aren't afraid. That's who I like to work with and will get results in my program.

So, I think about that person and create all of my messaging like I'm talking to that person. Their frustrations from working really hard but not getting results. It's more than just about money for them. You need to think beyond demographics and more about the psychographics of your ideal client. You want to courageously talk to that person in everything you do; through your funnel and in your actual launch. You'll be surprised at how they come out of the woodworks when you do that.

And you also repel the wrong people which is a great advantage! Because you don't want to waste your time and resources serving the people who aren't the right fit for you.

Top Tips for Launching Success:

- Understand the client journey at a very detailed level: from your ad or social media post all the way to being a client. For example, once I click that ad, what happens? Make sure you map out what that looks like.

- Know your numbers. Live Launches are a numbers game and knowing them is the first step to pinpointing the bottlenecks and dialing it in. For example, maybe your ads are converting well but they don't make it over to your actual launch event, or open your email, or make it to your Facebook Group. So, you can really start to see the small tweaks that you can make once you have the data. If you don't know your numbers, use the industry average.

- Make sure you have enough people at your Launch. I usually tell people not to launch unless you have at least 300 people because so much of it is your energy and the energy of your audience and your mindset. And if you don't have the audience, it's hard to hold your energy.

So, get a plan in place, get people registering for your launch and know your numbers!

The Most Important Metrics

We can get really nitty gritty with this, and eventually you should. But right now, if it's just you wearing all the hats you want to keep an eye on these:

1. **Sign-up rate** - how many people sign up?

2. **Butts in seats** - the number of people consuming the content. How many people are showing up live and watching the replay?

3. **Number of people taking your call-to-action** - how many people are buying or booking calls in with you?

Start at the very beginning with how many people are signing up, to how many are engaging and finally how many are taking action.

The Future of Launches

There are so many different containers you can do a launch in (i.e., from 90-minute masterclasses to 5-day challenges). I would recommend coming up with the content first and then matching the container to that so that people get what they need to make the buying decision.

You may find that you need to make some changes based on your audience. For example, we noticed that some markets have less time, so we've been shortening our launches. The bottom line is that launches will always be effective, it's just the details behind it that might change.

I don't see anything changing with actual launches because they're super effective! People love the human connection, they love the energy, they love the excitement of it, they love being able to come in and engage with other people. I don't see that going away especially as we get into a more and more automated world - human connection will become even more important!

The Live Launch Mindset

Mindset is the main thing I see when launches don't go well. I like to see people do a lot of launches before we try to really dial it in. Mindset is so important because you need to look at the long-game. If I had stopped after my first launch because I decided that I can't do high-ticket or that launching doesn't work, then I wouldn't be here today.

So, look at launching over the course of 12 months - that by the end of 12 months you're going to have your launch dialed in - versus needing to have it work the first time out of the gate.

Also, have the mindset that this is a learning experience and that you're going to learn so much rather than being attached to the result. This is really what takes most entrepreneurs out of the game!

It's the reason why so few people are truly successful, because it takes a particular type of person to make entrepreneurship work. You have to be in it for the long haul.

Melissa helped guide me through the launch and growth of our first coaching business, The Growth Boss. Just like Melissa, our first launch was not successful, but since then we have used this strategy to make multiple-6 figures. And we will continue to use the Live Launch strategy for all the reasons that Melissa has outlined - it creates a connection with your audience, it allows you to serve them, and as a result the right people *will* want to follow you into the sale. Approach it with the right mindset, and you too can find success with this LACE.

In saying this, when we made the next transition from The Growth Boss into Capsho and selling software, I knew there was something different we needed to add to our arsenal, which is where the webinar funnel comes in.

The Webinar Funnel with Vince Green from ClickFunnels

You might have noticed that just like with Dana Derricks, Melissa was inspired and mentored by Russell Brunson. By this time, I was also a user of ClickFunnels and had devoured all of his books. Being the Co-founder of one of the largest non-VC backed software companies in the world, I knew he was someone I could learn from and follow a lot more closely for the growth of Capsho.

And so, I did, and we made our next investment into his coaching program. His signature LACE is the Webinar Funnel - a 90-minute presentation that attracts your buyers and converts them. He credits this strategy for the growth of ClickFunnels, and so I knew this was what we had to make work next.

The Webinar Funnel is incredibly simple in strategy and is fully outlined in Russell's *Expert Secrets* book /available at www.deirdretshien.com/resources]. This is how it essentially works:

1. Based on your offer, what can you share about? The structure Russell recommends is to have five main components to what you're presenting: 1) Origination Story, 2) Your vehicle/framework, 3) Address and knock down the internal struggle they may have, 5) Address and knock down the external struggle they may have, 5) Make your offer and close.

2. Invite people to register for your webinar. As your participants are waiting for your webinar, how can you keep them engaged and excited about showing up live to your webinar? For example, we've tried things like extra training and incentivizing them with a live demonstration of how Capsho could work for their account.

3. Hold your webinar and make your pitch.

4. Follow up with the replay until your cart closes for the week.

This is a strategy that we have recently launched and are dialing in.

For this reason, I invited Vince Green, the Director of Coaching at ClickFunnels, to speak about the strategy. This is how he started:

In 2013 I retired from corporate life, yes it was basically my life. Prior to that day, the fact that I was living my life to build someone else's business was not sitting well with me anymore.

When I accepted that and then found myself in a moment where I had to make a personal commitment to myself so deep, so critical that this would become my new identity I chose to become an entrepreneur.

The allure was deep for me in the entrepreneur's world. Outside looking in it seemed easy. Oh boy was I in for an awakening. You see there was no going back because my commitment to myself was true. It was the way I would realize my personal, spiritual and economic freedom.

The one belief that crumbled fast was that being the entrepreneur, carrying the identity of the entrepreneur, living the life as an entrepreneur would merely be a matter of stating it. Not true. Neither would it prove to be easy.

The truth of the commitment was real. That meant I needed a model. I required frameworks and a guide that I could work for me to realize my goals.

The epiphanies to that uneasy situation were arriving fast with excruciating impact.

The talents that served me as a corporate guy are not going to serve me as an entrepreneur. I was a lone wolf.

All of my reach, the people I knew, the people in my network were behind me.

My trust and authority were behind me.

The ships were burned. I must move forward.

I needed new talents, which I define as skills, knowledge and experience, to become the successful entrepreneur.

I needed to map out the journey. First things first. What skills & knowledge did I need to build a business that would set me up for marketing and sales success?

This is where the first ironic moment landed.

I needed a webinar!

A webinar is the perfect vehicle to establish your credibility, trust and authority in your space. It allows you to demonstrate your ability to deliver the results your audience desires.

A webinar that people share with their peers, spouse or team. A webinar so compelling it filters your ideal customers from that big net we call Marketing.

When you can be in front of people to clearly articulate the journey from where they are, who they are to what they will achieve and who they become you will have their attention for as long as you need it.

The Webinar Strategy

In 2014 I decided to build software which would solve a level 8 problem within the industry I retired out of. I'm not a coder, but I was naive and lucky enough to find some great coders to work with me. If you build software, have a coder as a founding partner.

I had big plans. We validated the problem in the market. Built a desktop, mobile and cloud application. We were ready.

As we went to the market, reaching out to one business at a time, we did very well with those we knew and knew us. The relationship was solid. They bought because we were able to demonstrate the new way to manage an inventory segment they could only dream of.

As we ran through all those relationships sales stalled. One to one was not working. People would not reply to email. Phone calls become unanswered messages. Content was downloaded, not likely consumed. Our call to action was one to one demonstrations.

That should have been the wow that milked the cow.

But it wasn't. There is so much risk in being first to buy, or alone in buying a new product. That was our excuse anyway.

We were playing the old way. The corporate way.

In the world of direct response marketing, webinars are done one to many. One to many seemed to make more sense than one to one. That interested me.

If I was going to succeed as an entrepreneur, I would need new skills for presenting "one to many" webinars.

One of the mentors I found was Russell Brunson. I devoured his Dotcom Secrets book. We implemented so much of his funnel strategy it was starting to increase our list. Content and thought leadership need conversion to the list which leads to email marketing.

He had one more offer that intrigued me. It's the Perfect Webinar.

Bold name I thought. OK, what's the secret sauce to the webinar system?

Turns out it's all about presentation structure, frameworks, stories, strategies and case studies.

He is able to communicate in the webinar through all of those elements how he was able to get the results for his businesses. He was all about "show, don't tell".

Businesses, entrepreneurs and artists who need or want what you have are buying your frameworks to get the results you have shown others have achieved.

They remember the stories you tell them, in fact when those stories are memorable, they share them with others.

In every great webinar, the offer is what they buy.

Your offer, the offer that contains the frameworks, systems and processes is the "aspirin in the jam" that is their path to getting their results.

Your opportunity is to document and develop the frameworks, strategies and stories. Organize those assets into webinars using the Perfect Webinar.

The Most Important Components of a Webinar

Great webinars – webinars that convert – start with an invitation that generate a lot of curiosity. Webinars key in on the desire for the results that you can teach them to achieve or deliver with your service. People show up because of their self-interest and because they are curious about what you are going to share. Curiosity holds attention.

The question we are always answering is "What's in it for them?" Why should your ideal audience give you their attention, time and for some give you their money?

That age-old question is why they take in your article, blog, book, podcast, YouTube, conference, summit or every other piece of content or thought leadership you create.

They are looking for a solution to their problem without figuring it out on their own. What happens when they realize that you are not a relic from the past with the same old thing they have seen before? That you are fresh, insightful and are a real option for them … they want the next point of connection with you. They want to know if you, your team, and your services are for real.

I'll suggest they want to know if you can be trusted and are the authority in this space.

Some of you wear the "white coat" of authority but not all. That white coat carries you a long way but what if that is not the case for you?

Then I imagine you may be positioned as someone who is problem relevant. The person who went through what they are going through. Who didn't accept the current solutions in your space? Who developed frameworks, tools, systems or software which are now the go to solution in your space?

The truth about that is that it's new to them. You need to demonstrate the results. Show don't tell.

You're in that zone where doing these demonstrations one at a time is not scalable. You are not going to post your invitation up to a platform and hope the algorithm will get your message in front of the right people.

No. You are going to take charge of your own marketing and sales. You create content and thought leadership that attracts your ideal prospect.

Throughout the marketing you are inviting them to one place, one experience, one demonstration of your power - your webinar.

There are a few things that we do inside webinars, but the most important is telling stories. If you just have an improvement offer, if it's just 'bigger, better, faster', you could just do a feature comparison.

But when you have a new opportunity, you need to talk about it through stories because your audience has no idea what you do. You're not one of twenty different things that they could buy. You're actually just one of one. They've never seen it before so they need to know things like "what's the framework?", "What is it based upon?", "How did you learn it and earn it?", "where did it come from?", "What's the strategy?", "What am I supposed to be doing?".

And you need case studies!

In Russell's book *Expert Secrets*, he outlines one of the best ways to get case studies is to do training for free for a select number of people who are ready to buy. Perhaps you're giving away a free trial, training their team...

And all this time, you are *documenting* what's happening, the results they're getting, without giving away any of their trade secrets or private information. If you know you can get results for people, this is the best way for you to get those case studies.

In these case studies, you want to make it really clear what it is they wanted to achieve - for example, what did they want to achieve with Capsho? They want amazing content. Great! But what they also want is to create something high quality with less effort or less dollars spent.

And then how did it transform their business? One of the transformations might just be "hey we don't have to worry about this anymore! And I can now go apply my energy and time to something else."

This is at the core of what Russell calls the Perfect Webinar system.

How to Get Started with Webinars

Definitely grab a copy of *Expert Secrets* so that you can understand the Epiphany Bridge script, why we do trial closes and the 16 different closes that you can bring in.

It all starts with whether you can get results for your clients.

And then actually writing out your process. Don't just tell me, actually write it out!

This whole process is all about refining. If you just follow the rules, you're going to do ok. But then it's about making it your own, and that's the real change that needs to happen. How do you tell your stories in a way that elicits questions?

You must have:

- Your frameworks;
- How you earned it or learned it;
- Your strategy;
- Case studies

But outside of that, you don't have to have all your stories perfected! Apply the Epiphany Bridge script and go through the process of refining.

Practice and present with constant refinement until you become the leader in your market.

When practicing, use this framework to get the webinar dialed in.

1. Record the Webinar
2. Replay for Yourself
3. Refine the Gaps
4. Repeat 9 times

The first couple of times, record only the audio. Listen to the recording. Stop the recording and make changes to your slides, notes and bullet points.

Continue this refinement process with video and slides.

When you are comfortable that you are ready, invite a subset of your list to your webinar. Perform the full webinar with your offer. Give incredible bonuses rather than lowering the price. Over deliver as we like to say.

We have entrepreneurs using webinars for physical goods, courses, coaching, consulting, and even high-ticket events.

The Most Important Metrics

There are four key metrics:

1. **Registrations** - the conversion number of people who land on your page to those who register. Is there a magic number? On average, around 33% is what you'd want to be aiming for.

2. **Show-up rate** - you want to be aiming for around 50% of people who registered to show up for your webinar.

3. **Eyes on Pitch** - how many people are still on the webinar when you go into your offer stack and pitch them? It's not a bad thing to have people drop off when you're pitching because that's when people figure out that they may not be a good fit, and that's ok. This number will differ for everyone

4. **Sales** - around half of your sales will come from people on the webinar with you when you direct them to go to your sales page, and the other half will buy from your follow up. You'll get some emotional buyers straight on the webinar and you'll get more of the logical ones after.

The Future of Webinars

Webinars are essentially you telling your story about a new opportunity. This will never end. This is going to endure over time and stand on its own over a period of 20, 60 or 90 minutes. It can be broken up over sales letters and emails too. But at its core, you're telling stories. You're telling stories about how your strategy works, about how you discovered it, and how it worked for others.

There isn't an expiry date on telling stories because as humans, we're just wired that way!

You can start to see the trends coming up again and again with every person I speak to… tell stories, give, serve, fundamentally show up for your audience. I don't know anyone who has found any kind of success *not* credit these concepts. It's no wonder then that telling stories is core to the Honey Trap Formula.

Following Russell's exact webinar funnel and script, with Vince's coaching help (amongst others in the ClickFunnels team like Steve Bartetzko and Kyle Nussen) has helped me level up how I think about also approaching my Live Launch events and all of my other "sales" content, including emails, sales pages and content.

The Podcast Sales System with Josh Elledge from UpMyInfluence

As our own target Level 10 client and offer has been changing, so too has how we have needed to connect with them. I knew the power of the Live Launch Funnel and Webinars because that was how we had built our business. However, as our client type was changing - from entrepreneurs just starting, to CEOs looking to build a team to delegate social media crappiness - so were the number of them we could actually access through traditional means.

The higher our target Level 10 clients were becoming, the harder they were to find!

That was when I was introduced to Josh Elledge, Founder and CEO of UpMyInfluence. I went through his sales process and was amazed at how seamless the process was to converting me into a client! And I liked the different approach he was taking to engaging with his potential clients. Rather than focusing on attracting his dreamiest buyers by solving a problem they have (which is how the Live Launch and Webinar funnels work), it was centered around providing them with an opportunity to increase their status. This strategy and the next one (Viral Contests) are all about helping people increase their status.

Here's how the Podcast Sales System works:

1. Create a podcast based on what your dreamiest buyer would like to talk about *and* listen to.
2. Invite your potential dreamiest buyers (or Dream 100) to be interviewed on your podcast.
3. Use the interview time to build rapport and importantly, to show them in the best light possible.
4. When recording is complete, if they are someone you would like to build a further relationship with, suggest a follow up call to see how you may be able to collaborate.

Implementing this system has been an incredibly effective strategy for me to find and work with several (and counting!) Dream 100 collaboration partners. I had implemented it on the assumption that it was going to help me build my client base and I have instead been pleasantly surprised at the number of partnerships I've been able to build instead which - in all honesty - is worth more to me than signing up new clients.

This is why I invited Josh to share with you about The Podcast Sales System in his own words.

I got started on this completely out of necessity. My clients typically have become clients of mine through word-of-mouth and through building very personal relationships through networking. Everything I had ever experimented with in marketing typically just fell flat on its face.

I found that traditional marketing was great for attracting early-stage business owners but the problem I had was that early-stage business owners were just not going to be my ideal clients. They weren't ready to spend $1,000 or $2,000 a month on PR. That's not an early-stage business owner problem. At that stage, they're just going to do everything themselves.

So, anything I was doing around traditional marketing really just connected me with that earlier-stage business owner who was unwilling to make an investment like that.

I couldn't seem to get access to the higher stage clients through those traditional means.

So, I sat back and started thinking about how I generally accessed them. When I thought about my best clients and where they came from, I realized that it was always networking and at events - and it wasn't from the crowds! It was from the greenrooms, backstage.

Me just chatting with my peers was the best way for me to do business. Nothing even came remotely close!

But it wasn't scalable and there would be months at a time when I would get no new business. It wasn't sustainable.

So, what do I do? I started speaking multiple times a month, but I didn't want to become a road-warrior. Super inefficient.

The other option was that since I was already a really early adopter of podcasting with my previous business, why not make the investment in our podcast and start interviewing say three new people a week? These new people would fit the demographic and psychographic profile of my dream customer. I thought that if I just got them into the room and did something nice for them, that it might work ok.

And it did.

It took us a little while to get in the groove, but consistently doing about 3 interviews a week started leading people wanting to learn more about what we were doing, I would tell them and they'd sign on!

After a few months, ROI was amazing!

So that's all I do today. Today, I do 7 episodes a week and I'm always booked out 8 weeks in advance. And they're all with my dream customers. It is truly a joy to be able to network at this pace!

Why Podcasting is Exciting

The best part is that I don't have to sell. I can grow my company and I don't need to put the sales moves on anybody.

When we can have sales conversations that are very natural, that's the ideal! Especially for a non-salesy business owner or leader. It's the best not feeling the pressure to have to "convert" people. When you can just relax and say… "You know, this is a really great person. I'm happy to do something nice for them. We'll just see if something happens."

Now I am going to lead in that relationship in terms of talking about *potentially* what we could do together. I'm definitely going to bring that up. But that's pretty much it.

I like to treat sophisticated, successful, smart business owners as sophisticated and smart. We'll figure it out.

And when you're dealing with that much volume, you don't have to worry about anyone deciding to buy or not buy. If you're only talking to one person a week or two people a month, then you can get really hung up on whether they're to buy.

I really don't care. If they're a great fit, I get excited by that. If they're not a great fit, cool! What else can we do? How else can we help each other?

So, it's really about maximizing the value of the relationship, not trying to convert them into a singular outcome.

Getting Started

I think anyone can invite anyone to hop on a Zoom call. They're not going to do it if the premise of the call is a Discovery Call or a "free analysis". Everyone's always on edge with tactics like that.

There are two main considerations here:

1. If you want to sell high-ticket, you have to lead with giving first and coming to it with a generous mindset. I happen to believe that the podcasting platform is the easiest way to give. You have to fix your heart first. If your intention is to sell, it's not going to work. If your intention is to come together and see if you can do great work together, then you're going to do all right.

2. You need to make it ridiculously easy for these higher-level people to get to know you. If you're going to ask them to be a guest to be on a podcast, what are they going to need to know? Things like who your audience is and what questions you're going to ask. Invest in resources like short videos so that your guests develop familiarity bias.

The Most Important Components

The most important thing is that you have to lead with generosity. If I speak to someone where it's all about tactics and leads, it's a non-starter for me. Come back and talk to me in a year, after you get your nose bloodied some more.

Your brain and heart are not ready for what it takes to succeed in high-ticket sales today. If you have a Machiavellian view of sales, we all know it. You can continue to play the numbers game and spamming game. It's working less and less and you have to dump more and more money into ads.

It's not that business owner's fault by the way! We've just all been given bad information.

And well, we're all consumers, right? We change all the time! We've all become way more guarded, jaded and cynical to being sold to. For me, I just have such a low threshold for sales BS, cold emails, low-key selling on Facebook.

I know what's happening, every other successful business owner knows what's happening. And we don't like it.

Top Tips:

- When you're faced with the decision to either double down on the relationship or try to go for the "close" for the sale, double down on the relationship.
- Friends don't ghost friends. But we will do everything we can to not be sold at. So, if you don't make the sale but you preserve the relationship, you may lose the "battle" but you'll win the war. And the war really is the big picture.
- The big picture is you getting to the point when 500-800 people know you and wouldn't hesitate to recommend or refer you to somebody they know because you solve a very particular problem, it's game-set-match. You're pretty much set up for life.
- That should be what we're aiming for. Can you develop 500+ relationships within your community that wouldn't hesitate to connect you?
- This strategy isn't immediately going to set your world on fire, but if you're looking to make an impact through 2-4 high-ticket conversions a month and that's a great lifestyle for you, there's no better system on the planet.

The Most Important Metrics:

1. **Sales Conversion.** The number one metric you should always be on top of is sales conversion. You have to convert a sale, collect a credit card number, actually get paid.
2. **Number of Conversations.** Where does the sale come from? They come from conversations. If you know that generally, 15% of the people you talk to are going to buy, that means that approximately 1 out of 8 is going to buy - then you have to talk to 8 people as quickly as possible.

Now you can talk to 8 people in the space of 6 months, 2 months, 1 month or 1 week. You get to decide. The majority of people are not going to buy. You have to talk to everybody because there may be consolation prizes, but you want to get to that 15% that are absolutely going to buy. You just have to talk to more people! The more people you talk with, the more people you network with, the more sales you're going to get. The bottom line is that you have to increase the number of people you chat with.

The Future of This Strategy

It's only going to get better and better to lead with a relationship approach because marketers continue to ruin everything. Consumers are only going to get even more savvy.

Make sure you've created a system where you are a generous networker and create rooms where you are networking with the people who have the ability and desire to pay.

You may have noticed that once again, the same themes are appearing - giving, serving, leading with generosity.

The only difference with the Podcast Sales System strategy that Josh rightly points out is who this works for. If you are targeting higher-level clients who can't generally be found through just running ads or posting on social media, then this is a great strategy to get in front of the decision maker.

If you're not quite sure what LACE sounds best for you yet, but you want to get going with growing your list, then Viral Contests may be for you...

Viral Contests with Wilco de Kreij from UpViral

Viral Contests are one of the most effective ways to build your email list and social media following, and then get sales off the back of it. It's a strategy that I've employed ever since trying to grow The Choc Pot, and then Stax On Burgers, Baker Box NYC, The Growth Boss and now,

Capsho. And it has always worked wonders to grow my list (to the tune of 10's of thousands) and make sales!

Simply put, a Viral Contest is a mechanism to incentivize your dreamiest buyers to share about you to their network. Sharing can be done via email and/or via social media channels.

This is how it works:

1. You use the Traffic Pyramid (see previous chapter) to get traffic to your contest landing page.
2. Your contest will be something so awesome, it will compel people to sign up (more on this later).
3. Once they enter, they will be taken to another page that will outline all the ways they can earn more points to increase their chances of winning. A big component of this is to share the contest with their network, and it can also be by doing other tasks such as following you on your various social media channels.
4. You will want to continue nurturing this list right up until the contest ends so that you can maximize every opportunity for them to keep sharing.
5. Once the contest ends, you can make an offer to them to buy something so compelling that they would be silly saying "no"!

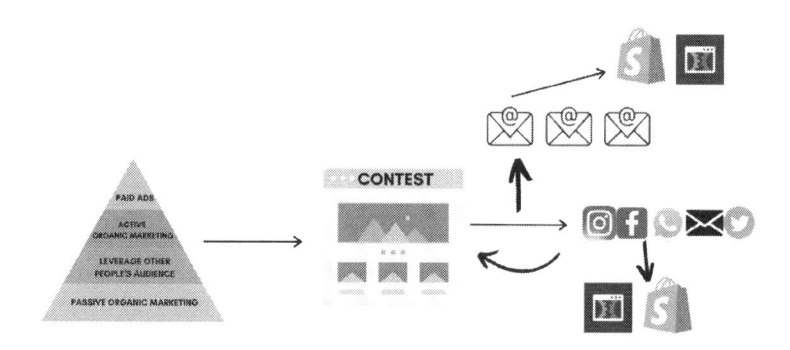

Can you see the beauty of this strategy? It is a completely gamified and viral way to attract new leads onto your list *and* create an opportunity to convert them!

When I used to run contests like these, we didn't have any software to help us do this quickly and easily. We would manually be entering people into spreadsheets and tracking their activities to determine the winner.

Now, I personally use a software called UpViral for any campaigns I'm running. And for this section, I invited Wilco de Kreij - the CEO & Founder of UpViral who has helped over 40,000 customers with their online marketing - to share his experiences and top tips running a Viral Contest campaign. The rest of this section on Viral Contests are in his own words:

Quite a few years ago, I had a business that was relying completely on Google AdWords. It was doing really well, but then Google changed their algorithm and, in an instant, all my traffic was gone. Literally overnight, I was back to zero.

At that point, I was thinking to myself… "What's next?"

I'm from the Netherlands and I love traveling. I had found myself living in Sydney a couple of times for a few months at a time and I thought… "Why not? It's my favorite city of all time!"

I had just finished University, and now had to "find a job". But instead, I booked a one-way ticket back to Sydney to enjoy life (and maybe do a little bit of work). I was renting a co-working space for about 6 months to give myself a deadline to make something work. However, whatever I tried just did not seem to be working!

At the time, I had no real list and was not selling any of my own products. But I was working on a side project where I had hired a bit of help to develop a specific plugin for Facebook.

And I thought… "this is pretty cool", so I created a landing page to offer this to other people because I had heard that the *money was in the list*.

And then on the Thank You page, I embedded a button that said "Share to Get" so people would have to share it on Facebook in order to then download it.

Because of that one tweak, I literally got thousands of shares. Mashable even wrote about this plugin! I had built an email list of a couple thousand subscribers. And that was when I realized the power of creating this virality.

Now I had this email list and I needed to work out what to do with it! I still wasn't selling a product or anything else at the time and I needed to put that email list to use.

So, I rehired the same developer to add some extra features to the plugin we had created and I created a "pro" version that people could upgrade into.

My aim with being in Sydney for those 6 months was to start something, but nothing had worked. Finally, on the very last day I was there, the "pro" version was ready, and just before boarding my flight back home, I sent an email to my database telling them about it. And literally in the first 12 hours, I did over $10k in revenue! This was when I first realized the power of incentivized sharing AND having an email list.

Incentives vs Contests

Even though I eventually founded a contest platform, I actually didn't start with contests - I started with *incentives*.

Incentives are when you get a prize for completing tasks (rather than being in the draw to win a prize). For example, it could be to refer 3 people and get access to a course. I've found that providing incentives has actually worked better in the B2B space. And people who use this strategy get a more consistent flow of leads.

Over time, I realized that contests have a fun factor and made it that much easier to get people to start sharing. People who use this strategy get big spikes of leads, rather than a consistent flow of leads. This strategy works best for B2C.

Coming Up with Your Contest Prize

If you're running a contest for the first time, I recommend that you give away your own product just so you can get started. I don't want you getting stuck on trying to figure out what prize to give away!

On the second time, I would recommend knowing your avatar. And then pick something that would specifically attract those people. For example, let's say you're selling a fishing rod and you decide to give away an iPad. Sure, people who are interested in a fishing rod may be interested in an iPad BUT those who are interested in iPads may not be interested in a fishing rod. Which means that you're getting people onto your list who will never buy from you.

You need to use your prize to automatically pre-qualify your leads. So, your prize should be very complementary to your product or to solve a problem that your ideal customer has.

It should be very specific to your avatar.

You also want to increase the value of your prize. This comes back to fundamental marketing principles around someone buying a drill - not because they want the drill - but because they want the hole in the wall.

When you talk about your prize, don't just say what it is (because people don't care about what it is), instead talk about what it will actually *do* for them.

For example, if you're giving away a coupon for a free dinner, you're not giving away a free dinner coupon, you're giving away a night out with your friends with drinks included!

Describe what it is actually going to do for them.

You want to make it exclusive. For example, if you're an author giving away your book, can you give away a signed copy? If you make shoes, can you do one in a different color just for the giveaway?

Create an experience around it. For example, if you're giving away a book, how about a meet-and-greet with the author too? If you have a restaurant, why not provide cooking lessons? These are things you would normally not be able to buy, and work great as prizes!

Coming Up with Your Incentive Prize

When running incentives, we actually tested two routes:

1. Share this with 3 friends and get this thing worth $197; and
2. You're 23rd in line. Share this with 3 friends to jump the queue.

Interestingly, we found that the second route got double the number of shares!

People weren't incentivized by getting something for free, they were incentivized by "beating" other people and being able to jump the queue. Have a think about how you might be able to use an incentive like this for your own referral program.

Promoting Your Contest

When promoting your contest, I recommend starting with channels you already know. For example, if you have a list, use that. If you already have social media, post it on there. If you already know how to run ads, use that.

For someone with absolutely no audience, think about what you have more of - time or money? If you have more money than time, then definitely run ads to your contest.

For people with more time, what I've seen work quite well are sponsorships. This is where I would reach out to other website owners [or Influencers/Dream 100] that already have traffic. I'd tell them I'm running a contest and if they could help us feature it via their social media or on their newsletter, then I'll promote them back. This works great when partnering with other small businesses also trying to get traction and build their audience as well.

If you reach out to 20, you might have 2 agree. This won't give you a huge amount of traffic but you just need to get some traffic in and once they start sharing, that will start to grow your list.

In return, you promote them back, potentially through a custom action to follow them on Instagram in UpViral or through your own social media and newsletter. So that way it's a win-win! And next time you run a contest; you'll have an even bigger list which means you can go after bigger [Dream 100] because you have this asset.

Top Tips to Incentivize Those Referrals

- *Instant gratification* - it's great to have a grand prize, but offer something they can unlock immediately if they just refer 3 people for example. That means that even if they don't win, they get something straight away.

- *Email follow ups* - a lot of people don't share straight away. Even if they do, you want them to keep doing it. In these emails, it isn't just about telling them to share, but why. Why should they share? What's in it for them? What are the stories you can tell about the impact it could have for them to share? People don't usually share for the sake of getting something, they share because they believe in it.

Important Metrics to Monitor

The most important metric to be monitoring for your contest or incentive is the *opt-in conversion rate*.

If you have a low opt-in conversion rate, it means that you're not explaining it well and that your copy needs to be looked at.

You may get a good conversion rate from people you're sending your contest to directly (your warm and hot audience), but if your copy is not on-point, you will find that whoever they share with (your cold audience) will likely not convert.

If you can nail this, it will have the biggest impact for you.

The Future of Contests

This will always remain because contests are based on human psychology. The channels might change, however the mechanism will not.

Ever since finding out there was an effective and efficient way to run contests and incentives using UpViral, I have launched them over and over again with my businesses and my client's businesses and have been amazed at the results!

We are now currently testing using both Contest and Incentive strategies. We will have incentives as an evergreen feature in our funnels, and run contests every quarter or biannually.

Be as creative as possible and think about where and how you can use these strategies as well!

If you'd like to sign up for an UpViral trial, you can access our affiliate link at www.deirdretshien.com/resources.

Which Strategy is Right for You?

You may be tempted after reading what you just have to want to *go do all the things*. Let me pause you for a second here and back that truck right up.

Trust me… from someone who has also done that, that doing it all is NOT the most effective way for you to grow your business and make money.

In fact, I was so mired in doing everything at once, that I burned out. I came out of that 2-day burn out at the beginning of 2022 with a new word for the year: Simplification.

Let me tell you a little about it…

We had grown our original coaching business, The Growth Boss, by learning from Melissa the Live Launch Funnel. We were running one every 4-6 weeks and had built a multiple 6-figure business using that strategy.

When we made the transition away from just helping e-commerce business owners - to helping entrepreneurs find their remarkability and taking the crappiness out of content creation for them - we knew we couldn't just rely on the Live Launch strategy.

Armed with our software product, Capsho, we didn't know if we wanted to be selling a high-ticket program any longer. And we only really knew the Live Launch Funnel as the vehicle to help us sell a high-ticket program.

Which meant we had to find a new way. That is how we started learning directly from Russell Brunson and his team of coaches about running Webinar Funnels.

Using the Webinar Funnel is how we launched our Grow My Podcast Accelerator offer. The Grow My Podcast Accelerator is for experts who podcast looking to grow their show . They may be a little newer to podcasting and have the time and will to learn it all and implement themselves.

However, during this time, there was still an unresolved loop running in the back of my mind.

I couldn't completely let go of the thought of having some form of high-ticket program because I truly believed in the efficacy of them. High-ticket programs are hands-down the best way to help clients get the results they are looking for… as long as they show up and do the work of course!

Having thought at this time about who our Level 10 clients were for our high-ticket offer, we knew we ideally wanted to work with people who were more progressed with their business, knew the value of their time and were ready to step into the role of being a true CEO and Chief Sloth Boss.

That was when we created the Capsho CEO offer. For entrepreneurs who want a complete podcasting and social media system plugged into their business. **Because** part of the offer was going to train a Virtual Honey Trap Assistant to do these activities for them.

And so, we launched this offer through a Live Launch Funnel.

So, by this time, we had a Webinar Funnel running to Grow My Podcast Accelerator and a Live Launch Funnel running to Capsho CEO.

Two distinctly different vehicles selling into two distinctly different offers.

In my mind, this made sense. Reality, however, was a different story.

After only a few weeks of going back and forth pitching two different offers, which meant finding and speaking to two distinctly different audiences, I found ourselves quickly burning out.

In the space of two days - the first day feeling pretty good about what we had built and were implementing, and the next day feeling completely overwhelmed and exhausted, I knew that things had to change.

We had to strip it right back and go back to basics. What were we looking to do with our business? What was the future of our business and where did we therefore need to spend the majority of our time and effort?

Bona and I had to have a serious discussion about this. As our COO and in charge of fulfillment for our clients, my ask of Bona was simple: If we knew that the future of this business was going to be driving Capsho the software, which program were we best positioned to scale? Grow My Podcast Accelerator or Capsho CEO?

The answer? The Accelerator. Because of course, a higher-ticket offer like Capsho CEO takes up a lot more of our time, headspace and bandwidth.

In addition, finding a lot of our ideal Level 10 clients, while not impossible, was going to be very hard from a volume perspective - just like what Josh found. And we were becoming more and more convinced that the best way to find and convert them would be through a higher touch relationship-based funnel.

And so, we started simplifying. We believed in both the Webinar and Live Launch Funnels to be incredibly effective LACE's to attract and convert clients. But instead of trying to use them to pitch two different things, we decided to use them to pitch the *same thing*. Grow My Podcast Accelerator .

And instead of trying to sell one-to-many into our Capsho CEO program through the Live Launch Funnel, I implemented Josh's Podcast Sales System to not only create relationships with potential Capsho CEO clients - but more importantly - my potential Dream 100 collaboration partners.

And throughout, I weaved in elements of Viral Contests and Incentives.

As a result, we were able to simplify our front-facing messages to just one type of client and one type of offer. Simple.

I don't tell you this whole journey to convince you to implement *all of it*. In fact, I'm telling you this for the exact opposite reason.

To hopefully save you from yourself (like I needed saving from *myself*) and help you focus on just one vehicle to begin with. To save you from a potential future burn out.

So, let's start there… What is the best vehicle or funnel for you?

What Vehicle or Funnel should you start with?

Regardless of what you sell - coaching, consulting, services, products - you need a LACE. You need a way to not only attract your leads, but to also convert them. This should be the primary conversion event you focus on.

Anything else? Other lead magnets you create, your website, any other sales pages… they should just be bonuses on top.

Because given the choice in where to spend your time and energy driving traffic - I will *always* recommend spending it on your LACE. Again, this is something that is not only going to be attractive to your audience, that is, provide them with something of value. But it will also be a means by which you can lead them into a sale.

When it comes to deciding which vehicle or funnel you start with, you need to approach it from the perspective of your dreamiest buyer. What would *they* likely be attracted to? What would *they* show up for? How would *they* convert?

The reason why we decided to move away from the Live Launch Funnel for Capsho CEO is because our dreamiest buyers in this offer just wouldn't have the time to spend an hour over consecutive days to attend a Challenge or Bootcamp. It's not something they would be attracted to.

But what would be potentially attractive to them is the prospect of increasing their authority and status through a Podcast Funnel. And this way, I get to have a genuine conversation about whether we might be a good fit to work together in some way.

However, the Grow My Podcast Accelerator client who has more time than they probably do money, will find the time to attend a multi-day training. It's something they are more likely to be attracted and show up to.

And our aim with our Grow My Podcast Accelerator clients is to ensure that they are *so successful* that they will need our Capsho CEO program.

And at that point, it becomes a no-brainer for them to continue their journey with us.

If you find yourself in a similar situation, targeting people who are more likely to have the *time*, then the Live Launch and Webinar Funnels are highly recommended.

If you are in a much more relationship-based business, perhaps selling a high-ticket service or consulting offer, the Podcast Sales System may be your best option.

If you are a product-based business, I have seen the most success with Viral Contests.

Now that you may have an idea of which vehicle or funnel you are going to start with, how do you make it your own?

How Do You Make It Your Own?

When I refer to making it your own, I'm actually referring to the fact that it's possible to merge, mold and create variations of any of these funnels and vehicles to suit your business and your dreamiest buyer.

For example, we have had much success in the e-commerce space with a variation of both the Live Launch and Webinar funnels.

This is something we used to teach called the Live Conversion Method, where you sell your products Live online. This strategy is what propelled our clients like Danesa and Janet into running 6-figure businesses. If you are interested in learning more about the Live Conversion Method and how to apply it to your e-commerce business, check out my book The Conversion Formula, available through www.deirdretshien.com/resources.

I have similarly made different variations on each of the different funnels to make them my own.

For example, the traditional Live Launch funnel is a 5-day Challenge. While we started with 5 days, we have also done 3 & 4-Day ones. We will also be experimenting with a 30-Day Challenge.

Another example is with the Podcast Sales System. I have tweaked and molded it into something I now call The Celebrity Funnel.

I deliberately call this The Celebrity Funnel because this is how I am looking to build up the "celebrity" of my podcast guests.

As Josh previously mentioned, this strategy is anchored in serving and creating conversations. If it happens to come up that what we offer is something they're looking for, awesome. If it isn't, then I know we can find another way to collaborate. Hence why it is also such an effective Dream 100 strategy.

And throughout this funnel, I am intentional in seeding what it is we do and incorporating other elements such as Viral Incentives.

The Celebrity Funnel is something we now teach inside Capsho CEO.

Once you start focusing on implementing the one vehicle or funnel you have decided to start with, you *will* find ways to make it your own.

Focus on the value you want to be providing your dreamiest buyers, and the rest will come.

Setting Your Launch Date

Getting the first one kicked off is always the hardest part to implement. It is relatively easy to theoretically think and talk about something, and yet, when it comes to actually launching it, it is easy to let all of the fears stop you.

You may think it's because you don't have the time, or you may call it perfectionism. Ultimately, it comes down to fear of rejection or failure in some form.

We could spend a *long* time trying to work through this. What I would say in short is that we *all* suffer from variations of this. And literally the only way to get over it is to work *through it*.

That is, don't ignore it. Acknowledge it for what it is but *decide to do the scary thing anyway*. And that means setting the launch date of your LACE and doing everything you can to make it happen.

Will it work the first time? Maybe, maybe not. It didn't for me, it didn't for Melissa, it didn't for Dana. Literally anyone successful I've spoken to; it never worked the first time.

That's not the point. The point is to do it anyway. Do it anyway without any expectations of achieving a specific result. Do it anyway from the place of wanting to serve your audience. Approaching it this way will get you the sales and the income you're looking for!

7.
DOING IT ALL WHILE SPENDING ONLY 2 HOURS PER WEEK ON SOCIAL MEDIA!

If you've made it this far in the book, congratulations! You really are the top 1%. I know that while *I* might find this whole topic exciting, it's not for everyone…

We're on the home stretch! This chapter is all about how you can now take everything you've just learned and do it all… while only spending 2 hours a week on your total social media activities.

When I started this book, I promised you that once you knew the entire strategy, I would also unveil how you Sloth Bosses can then implement all of this while only spending 2 hours of your week on social media activities.

And being able to do that comes down to the bonus component of The Honey Trap Formula - systemization and delegation…

$$\$\$ = \frac{M + C + T + L}{S + D}$$

The Delegation Mindset

I know firsthand how hard delegation is. It may be for a variety of reasons. Perhaps it's being a "perfectionist" and thinking you will need to spend more time reviewing than if you were to do it yourself. Perhaps it's being a "control freak" knowing that no one else will be able to do the things as well as you can. Perhaps if you're like me, it may be because you're addicted to work.

However, are any of those the *real* reason?

I'd like to take this opportunity to offer another potential reason. A deeper one. Because this is something I also struggle with.

And that is because you may be ***playing it small***.

I thought that I was past this myself, but I only recently realized that I'm in fact not.

And I wouldn't blame you for thinking "Surely! Deirdre with her years and years being an entrepreneur and building multiple-6 & 7 figure businesses would not be playing it small!"

I can assure you that this is a chronic problem for me.

I get asked all the time whether I have any regrets or whether I would have done anything differently in my time. And the immediate thought that used to pop up was that I wish I hadn't started my entrepreneurship journey in hospitality. Because it was *hard*.

It was financially hard, it was emotionally hard, it was physically hard.

I also know *now* that I wouldn't have had it any other way. It is because of how hard it was that I had to make gigantic leaps before I was ready.

For example, with it being financially hard - and being on the hook with debt and lease agreements - meant we had no choice but to make it work.

With it being physically hard meant we had no choice but to have a team and learn to delegate from Day 1.

Which meant that in many ways, we were thankfully forced to get out of our own heads and just do it.

However, as I said, it's still a chronic problem for me.

So fast forward to starting an online business, it took me a *long* time to bring a virtual assistant (VA) on. Even then, when it was absolutely necessary, I still didn't feel ready. Having an online business lulls, you into this false sense that it's easy to do *everything*. To the point that I had no idea what we were actually going to get her to do.

I didn't have anything systemized, I didn't know if there was going to be enough hours for her in the work, I didn't know if we were going to be able to promise her ongoing work. But we did it anyway.

And the same thing happened time and time again, with our second and third and fourth VA.

Now, you may excuse me for thinking that I now have this handled - that I am no longer playing it small - and yet, this chronic problem follows me *every time* I am trying to level up.

This will likely happen for you too. I can pat myself on the back and congratulate myself for making these seemingly big decisions and taking these big steps, and yet, what I fail to keep remembering is that there is going to be another one literally just around the corner.

So, let me tell you about my most recent experience which made me realize that this journey is never ending.

When we developed our first iteration of the Capsho software, we knew it was going to be rudimentary - it was an alpha version after all, something to get out there, get tested and see if it was something our audience even wanted.

The great news is that it was!

So now came decision time. Do we keep playing it safe and use the same cost-effective development agency, even though we knew they wouldn't be able to bring to life the true vision we had for Capsho?

Or do we invest in bringing a Chief Technology Officer into the team to take us where we needed to? Invest in higher level thinking?

Seems like a simple decision when I put it like that, doesn't it?

And yet it wasn't. All of the same fears came up for me. What if we run out of money? What if we don't get any new customers? What if everyone hates it? What if I let the whole team down and they won't have jobs any longer?

At least if we made the "smart choice" to stay within our very defined modest budget, then we could give ourselves more runway while we "keep testing". And then once we make $X or $Y or hit this milestone or that milestone, *then* we can make the investment.

Do you see what I'm doing here? Already, I'm defaulting to playing it small. And rationalizing it logically.

Does it sound familiar? Do these things come to your mind too?

Trust me, I get it. And it hits me every single time I need to level up.

It took me a couple of months to take a deep breath, close my eyes and make the gigantic leap.

Now, I can literally *feel* the difference in me and in my business. Because I forced myself to level up, and by doing that there's no turning back.

It's been determined, it's been ordained, that this business is going to grow and scale beyond our wildest imagination. It just is.

Because *I'm* growing beyond my wildest imagination.

And THIS is what I've now realized is the one thing that sets successful entrepreneurs apart. They may know the fear, they may feel the fear, and yet they take that courageous step forward anyway.

So that they are no longer playing it small. And this is something I would encourage anyone reading this to do too.

How? Delegate. And I don't just mean by delegating down. I mean delegate up *and* down! Delegate up through investing in higher-level thinking. For me, it was in bringing a very experienced CTO into the team. For you, it could be investing in a coach or a mentor. You've already seen proof in this book how much I invest in higher-level thinking to keep pushing me to stop playing small. You must start doing that too.

And also, yes, delegate down. There is no point in investing in higher-level thinking if you *don't have the time or energy* to actually implement it all yourself. This is where I see a lot of people who have come through my own programs and other programs fail. There is just no way unfortunately that you are going to see the type of results I know you're looking for - implementing *any* strategy or program - without support on the ground. I've tried it and it doesn't work.

Regardless of where you are in your business, this *is* possible for you! So, let's stop playing small and level up together! Let me hold your fear for you as you take a deep breath, close your eyes and take a gigantic leap forward into…

The Delegation System

When I first started writing this chapter, I was actually in bed on a cold winter morning. I had this habit of getting up just before 6am and spending an hour writing. On this particular morning in January, it was just too cold to get out of the warm cocoon under the covers, so I instead started typing it out on my phone.

As I was writing, and just letting all the thoughts get out of my head, I suddenly typed something out that made me stop… without even knowing or thinking about it, I had typed "I myself have a deep-rooted addiction to working."

I had never once ever thought or considered this a possibility, but there you go. The longer I thought about this topic (and discussed it with Bona on The Remarkable Entrepreneur's Playbook podcast), the more I knew this to be true.

You now know my past, know how driven I am – academically when I was growing up and as an entrepreneur now. It's not surprising given all of that and how I've been rewarded and validated all my life that I am addicted to working.

I feel guilty if any part of my day is not productive. It is how I've always believed I add value to those around me. It's about the only thing I've ever been praised for. It's ultimately where my self-worthiness comes from.

The more I thought about it, the more I knew that how I found myself to be "worthy enough" was in direct proportion to how much I worked and the number of tasks and projects I was able to complete.

Which is what made *this* particular journey - systemization and delegation - a little bit more difficult.

The most cited book for the need to systemize and delegate is *the E-Myth Revisited* by Michael E. Gerber. In it, he tells the story of a baker, Sarah, who spent all of her time as the technician in her business, not as an owner and entrepreneur. As he says, "if your business depends on you, you don't own a business, you have a job. And it's the worst job in the world…"

I think almost all of us who start businesses - and happen to be addicted to work - know this feeling.

And as a recovering workaholic, letting go of being the technician is really hard. In fact, it's something I'm still working on.

It was only very recently that it hit me how important doing this is.

We had worked with a Virtual Honey Trap Assistant (VHA), Grace, for over 12 months and had just brought on an additional two VHA's as well (almost by accident actually!)

With these additional resources, we decided to not only delegate the tasks we knew we wanted to, but we could start actually giving them responsibility for more. For things we weren't even doing yet, like TikTok content creation and YouTube content creation. On top of removing a lot of tasks we just *did not want to do*.

And suddenly… I found myself able to breathe.

And when I was finally able to breathe, I was able to think. And not just think about the day-to-day activities, but to start thinking *creatively*.

Creativity (I soon realized once I was able to tap into more) is important for *all* aspects of your business. It helps you with better problem solving, it helps you with better content creation, it helps you think outside of the box, and interestingly it actually becomes an energy source, feeding you with more as you feed it.

As the CEO and face of your business, you not only have to protect your time, but your energy. You're the one who has to show up for your audience, connect with them, engage with them, ultimately *sell* to them. If you don't protect your energy, you don't have a sustainable business.

Creativity feeds your energy.

So how do we create this creative energy? The *only* way is to get more off your plate, which is through systemization and delegation.

With that in mind, let's start at the very beginning…

Who Should You Delegate To?

I have tried multiple models in my time building businesses, and for an online business just starting to grow, an overseas Virtual Honey Trap Assistant is hands down the best place to start.

I've found them (generally) to be loyal, capable, open to feedback and the best part? Cost-effective. This is such an important consideration when it comes down to making your first few hires because creating large overheads in wages and salaries can very quickly sink a growing business.

I've been down that path and let me tell you, it is an *incredibly* expensive exercise!

So, let's at least make the courageous decision to at least dip our toes a little in first. And the best way to do this is by starting with offshore support.

Let's cover an important question: What the heck is a Virtual Honey Trap Assistant?

A Virtual Honey Trap Assistant (VH A) is someone who is going to help you implement the strategies in this book. They are going to do all the heavy lifting to implement The Honey Trap Formula so that you are only spending 2 hours a week on all of your social media activities!

How? Let's take a closer look at what you can and more importantly, should, delegate.

What Should You Delegate?

A lot of people make the mistake of looking to only delegate administrative tasks to their Virtual Assistant (VA). And while we logically know that this is a worthy exercise, it is also a hard one to justify sometimes because well… you could just as easily do these tasks yourself! In fact, you already have. Yes, it will be painful for you and will take up your time, but at least it's not costing you anything financially, right?

It is for this exact reason that I encourage everyone to not hire a VA, but to hire a VH A instead. Someone who is going to *directly contribute to your top line sales.*

How are they going to do that? By taking carriage of a couple of the components of The Honey Trap Formula for you, namely "C" and "T" - creating your content to help you build your credibility and authority and by actually implementing the Traffic Pyramid to grow your audience and source leads for you.

What might this look like? Let's break it down.

Content Creation (the "C")

I'll take you through the 3 activities YOU need to be doing for your content creation. Everything else? Your VH A will be doing.

> 1. Be the Talent - the first activity you will be responsible for is to be the talent. As the face of the business, this activity is mandatory. And it's going to be a *lot* easier than you think! Because you VH A will be doing all the Content Hacking and will propose - to you - the concepts they have for your next 9-grid of posts. And all you'll have to do is to go through it with them, agree on the content to be created (this

should take you 30 minutes), and then go ahead and create those photo, video, reel, TikTok content (this should take you another 30 minutes)! Once you have the raw files, you just give them to your VH A to make all the edits according to the look and feel of your brand. In under an hour, you've created the creatives for your posts!

2. Share Your Story - I've already the foolproof, no-brainer way for you to share your story in under 5 minutes. Put your story into Capsho. In fact, if you already create some type of long-form content where you share your story (e.g., a Facebook live, a podcast, a YouTube video, a blog), then your VH A can complete Capsho for you. If not, you know now it will only take 5 minutes for you to complete! And from Capsho, your VH A will have a whole *bank* of captions available for them to use. This will give you your draft captions based on your long-form content .

3. Review & Provide Feedback - With the creatives and captions, your VH A will now have what they need to pull together a draft 9-grid of posts for you. You will make any edits to the captions, which will take less than 30 minutes to do. Once everything has been reviewed by you, your VH A will schedule your content to post.

And that's it! The whole process for you to spend less than 2 hours a week creating content for your social media. And at the end of it you will have engaging and effective content. Nothing standard, nothing boring, all completely *you*!

See the next page for a visual aid of the process…

YOUR VHA / YOU

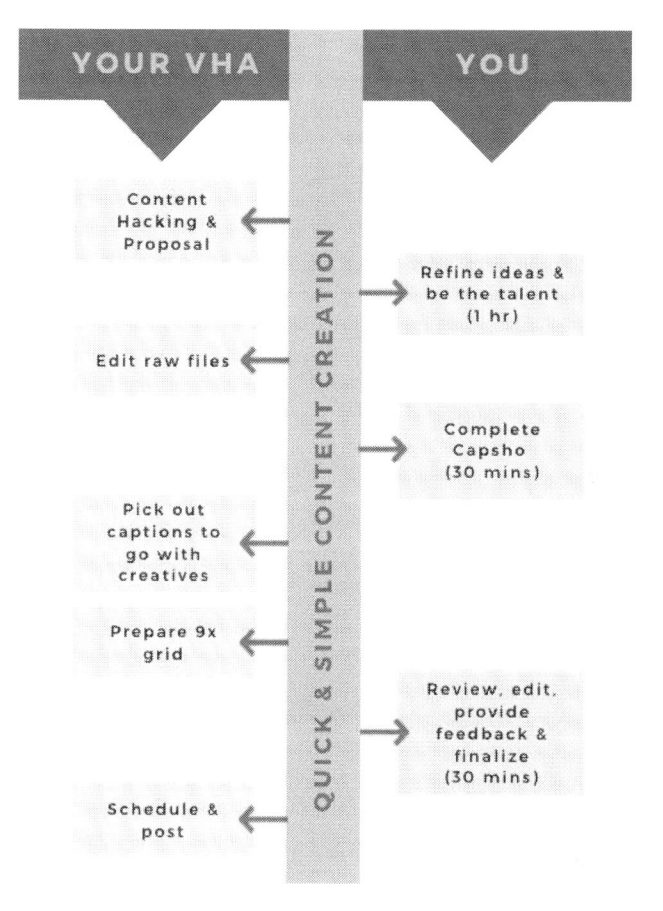

QUICK & SIMPLE CONTENT CREATION

YOUR VHA:
- Content Hacking & Proposal
- Edit raw files
- Pick out captions to go with creatives
- Prepare 9x grid
- Schedule & post

YOU:
- Refine ideas & be the talent (1 hr)
- Complete Capsho (30 mins)
- Review, edit, provide feedback & finalize (30 mins)

The Traffic Pyramid (the "T")

Creating your content is one part of what your VHA can do to help you with your Honey Trap Marketing. The other, very important part? The Traffic Pyramid.

I've already taken you through the strategy and process of each tier of the Traffic Pyramid, starting with Passive Organic Marketing, going into Leveraging Other People's Audiences, into Active Organic Marketing and finally Paid Ads.

Your VHA can track and optimize the data on your social media. They can find, engage and invite Influencers or Dream 100 into a potential collaboration call. They can also do *all* of the Active Organic Marketing outreach activities into your LACE.

While my VHA does not currently run my ads (although, it's only a matter of time!), they do help me with the creative part of it, especially as they can keep an eye on the type of content that is working organically.

Being able to delegate all of this has literally saved myself and Bona over 60 hours a week combined! And you may say… "but that's not possible. There's no way you were spending all that time on these activities before."

And you would be right. We weren't. We were not able to do much of these activities consistently at all! Which is why we needed a VHA! And so do you!

What about the rest of Honey Trap Marketing?

It's important to note that the "M" and "L" (Messaging and LACE) components of the Honey Trap Formula need to still sit with you. Because these are the fundamental *sales* components. Converting the leads your VHA is bringing in to become customers or clients of yours.

However, that is not to say they cannot support you in those activities. For example, one of my VHAs helps me with running all of my Live Launch Funnels.

Once you start with your first VHA, I guarantee you won't be able to stop because you'll start to think differently. Instead of asking yourself "what can I get my VHA to do?", you'll be asking yourself "what *can't* my VHA do?!"

How Should You Delegate?

When I heard Bona quote the author James Clear the first time, I knew this was someone I had to listen to. He said: "You do not rise to the level of your goals. You fall to the level of your systems."

And boy oh boy, I couldn't agree more wholeheartedly! Systems will be the make or break for your business. Trust me, I've lived them. Fortunately, I have a relatively structured mind when I spend a little bit of time thinking things through.

Which is why I've been able to systemize TWO businesses making multiple 7-figures in Sydney, and be able to physically leave them to run on their own. In fact, I'm amazed at how the systems have held up because moving over to NYC in 2019, we could not foresee that we would not be able to head back to Sydney for another *three years* due to Covid-19! And yet, through this time, not only has the business run itself, it has been able to grow!

So, what is the best way to delegate? It's a relatively simple 3-step process:

1. Shoot a video showing them how to do what it is you want them to do. The easiest way to do this is to actually complete the action, and just video your screen as you're talking through the steps and why out loud. Be as detailed as possible!

2. Once they have watched the video, have them do the activity themselves (with a real example), and shoot a video of themselves doing it. Watch it over and see if you have any feedback for them. If you do, provide them with your feedback.

3. Once they've done it a few times and you're confident in their ability to do the activity, have them create a Standard Operating Procedure (SOP) document detailing each step. This SOP and associated training videos now form part of your systems.

I have laid out for you the complete process to effectively level up through delegation - who to delegate to, what you should delegate and how to delegate.

However, this is just one part of the leveling up equation. This is the part that is externally driven and may be easy to "blame" if things don't go quite to plan.

What I find is that we can systemize and delegate all we like, but as the leader, we still have to shoulder the accountability and responsibility for the success of our business. The success of our business comes down, not just to having the right strategy and the right people, but also to ensuring we have the right habits.

So that we can do everything in our power, day in and day out, to do what we need to in order to nurture and grow our business. And doing the things we need to, day in and day out, comes down to the habits we form.

Which is why I now wanted to talk about building these habits…

Building Your Habits

I can't talk about building habits without referring, once again, to James Clear and specifically to his bestselling book Atomic Habits. In it, James shares his principle that habits are the compound interest of self-improvement. Mastery of anything - including Honey Trap Marketing - requires patience and small, daily contributions which appear to make no difference until you hit a critical threshold.

The delegation strategy and system I laid out in the previous section are only useful if you are able to integrate them into your business as daily and weekly habits and repeat them enough times until they become automatic.

Whenever you are trying to build a new habit, James suggests *Four Laws of Behavior Change* to making it stick:

The 1st Law - Make It Obvious

Once the initial motivation for starting this new system wears off, the thing that will keep it (and you and your VH A) going is how it has been designed into your day-to-day environment.

This first law is all about creating a cue to trigger the new behavior you are adopting to implement this new system with your VH A, and making this cue as obvious as possible.

For many of us, our calendars are our main workflow cues (if it doesn't get scheduled it doesn't get done!) So, making your new system obvious can be as simple as scheduling in each step of the content creation process, I covered in the previous section so that it is in your calendar as a must-do every week. For example, in my calendar I have:

- A Monday morning meeting with my VH A where she presents content proposals from her content hacking for us to refine together (30min)

- A Monday afternoon block to film footage for the content concepts we refined (30min)

- A Thursday morning meeting to review the final drafts of the content before it is scheduled and posted (30min); and

- A Sunday morning block for me to complete Capsho so the bank of captions stays fresh (30min)

Sometimes, an action we *already* take can be the cue for a new action we *want* to take. This is where habit-stacking comes in. Habit-stacking means taking a habit you already do and stacking your new behavior on top.

After I [current habit], I will [new habit I need to do]

For example, I have a weekly habit already in place of recording my podcast episodes on Sunday mornings (after pancakes!) It is when I feel most inspired to record and so I habit-stacked my new behavior of using Capsho straight after the podcast recording.

The 2nd Law - Make It Attractive

The second law to building habits that stick is all about the motivational force behind the habit. If we're not craving the change we need to make, we don't really have a reason to act. But the thing is, none of us are craving the new habit itself. We're craving the feeling we *anticipate* it will give us. The greater the anticipation, the greater our motivation to act.

One easy way to make your new habit more attractive is to use what James Clear calls temptation bundling. This basically means giving yourself a new rule where you pair something you need to do (the new habit) with something you want to do.

After [new habit I need to do], I will [habit I want to do]

With enough repetition, your brain starts to program itself to realize that doing what you *need* to do means you get to do the thing you *want* to do.

For example, I really don't enjoy being on camera. Unfortunately for me, part of my role as the face of the business is to take the raw footage my team needs to create our social media content. So, after I take the videos and photos the team needs me to as the 'talent', I will go for my weekly long walk which is one of my favorite ways to recharge my batteries.

Another powerful way to make your new desired behavior really attractive is to join a group where it is the normal behavior AND you really identify with this culture of the group. This will give you the external accountability and inspiration we all need to continue leveling up. For me, being surrounded by other amazing committed entrepreneurs inside Russell Brunson's Coaching program keeps me motivated. Similarly, the communities we have created to support our Capsho clients, plays a similar role for them. We share notes on how we are implementing the strategy, celebrate wins and also failures!

The 3rd Law - Make it easy

As someone who has always been very disciplined, I have noticed there is a pattern in how I approach mastering new things. I break the new thing down to what James Clear calls the "gateway habit". This is the very first and very *easy* step that will naturally lead you to your desired outcome. For example, if your goal is to write a book like it was for me, the gateway habit may be to write a sentence a day.

As soon as you are consistent and committed to this gateway habit, you can use 'habit shaping' to scale it up to your ultimate goal i.e., increasing the difficulty until you are able to comfortably do the 'hard thing'. So, in the example of writing a book, you go from writing a sentence daily, to a paragraph daily then a page daily until you have a full book in your hands!

Similarly, 'Implement Honey Trap Marketing for my business' can feel like a big, scary, hairy goal which feels impossible to accomplish. And

I can guarantee it will stay unaccomplished if the goal remains at that high a level. This is why our programs for our clients, I have mapped out this large outcome of implementing Honey Trap marketing into the required gateway habits and an implementation plan that scales them up the curve.

The 4th Law - Make It Satisfying

Whilst the first 3 laws of forming habits that stick will help you follow the process, I have laid out for you the first time, this law is what will help ensure you continue to do it. The cardinal rule of behavior change is that we repeat what is immediately rewarded. Change is easy when it's enjoyable. We're simple creatures always looking for instant gratification after all.

As entrepreneurs, there is nothing more satisfying than the feeling of making progress. A simple way to do this is to visually track your new habits - for each piece of the system I have laid out for you in the previous section - and challenge yourself to not break the chain.

This was an important realization for us when we found that even our most engaged and motivated clients were having trouble staying consistent with implementing Honey Trap Marketing. In redesigning our programs, we made sure our clients have a visual roadmap to track to and that each win, however little, is celebrated as they progress.

Success in any form, but especially in business, is not an end state we reach but rather an endless process that we continue improving every day. Make it obvious, attractive, easy, and satisfying. My hope is that you now have a much better system to truly set yourself up for the success you deserve.

SUMMARY

We've covered a lot in this book. Let's do a brief regroup and then I'll give you suggestions on how to best implement this information in your business.

- You know about *Honey Trap Marketing*, an experimental heart-centered approach to rapidly turning followers into buyers. You know how powerful implementing Honey Trap Marketing can be for the growth of your business.
- You know the importance of balancing stories and data at each component of your marketing. In this chapter, we will be covering the systems part of *Honey Trap Marketing*.
- You know that implementation of *Honey Trap Marketing* occurs through *The Honey Trap Formula*:

$$\$\$ = M + C + T + L$$

- You know each step of this formula now and how to implement it.
- You know how to come up with *Messages* for your dreamiest buyers, and then how to use Messagelytics to test for which one/s your buyers actually care about.
- You know how to create your *Content* anchored in the three fundamental pillars of creating your *Content Trust Accelerators*:

evoking emotions, storytelling and practical value. You also know how to create your *Content Honey Traps to create curiosity*.

- You know how to now get your *Traffic* through the 4 tiers of The Traffic Pyramid - Passive Organic Marketing (i.e., reading the data to have your content perform for you); Leveraging Other People's Audiences; Active Organic Marketing; and Paid Ads.
- You also know how to create a *Lead Attracting Conversion Event* - a vehicle for you to attract your leads AND convert them at the same time!
- You now know how to systemize and delegate it all!

So, we're at the end of our time together (for now!) Thank you so much for reading *Honey Trap Marketing*!

If you want more help and are ready to put what you've just learned into practice, then I'd love for you to reach out to me through www.deirdretshien.com.

ABOUT THE AUTHOR

Deirdre is the Co-founder & CEO of Capsho, software that helps Experts who podcast create their AI-generated episode title, player description, show notes, episode social media captions and email with Content Honey Traps so that they can grow their listeners!

She is the creator of Content Honey Traps, author of Honey Trap Marketing and host of the Grow My Podcast Show.

She is a serial entrepreneur, having founded and led 7 businesses across 5 industries in the last 9 years, and has navigated the entire spectrum of experiences and emotions (the good, the bad and the ugly) that comes with starting, running and closing businesses.

With her hands-on experience in successfully growing her businesses to 6 & 7 figures, she now coaches and works hands-on with experts who podcast to grow their audience using the Content Honey Trap System.

W: www.capsho.com & www.deirdretshien.com

IG: @deirdretshien & @capshohq

Podcast: www.growmypodcastshow.com

Made in the USA
Monee, IL
30 August 2023

32855050-c3b0-4951-8c3a-28329bc247a0R01